E-learning with Camtasia Studio

A step-by-step guide to producing high-quality, professional E-learning videos for effective screencasting and training

David B. Demyan

PUBLISHING

BIRMINGHAM - MUMBAI

E-learning with Camtasia Studio

First published: August 2014

Production reference: 1190814

Published by Packt Publishing Ltd.
Livery Place
35 Livery Street
Birmingham B3 2PB, UK.

ISBN 978-1-84969-866-5

www.packtpub.com

Cover image by Pratyush Mohanta (tysoncinematics@gmail.com)

Credits

Author
David B. Demyan

Reviewers
Jason R. Clemens
Richard M. Garetano
Sylvia Moessinger
Erika Smith
Travis Thurston

Commissioning Editor
Kunal Parikh

Acquisition Editor
Vinay Argekar

Content Development Editor
Arvind Koul

Technical Editors
Mukul Pawar
Siddhi Rane
Shruti Rawool

Copy Editor
Laxmi Subramanian

Project Coordinator
Neha Bhatnagar

Proofreaders
Simran Bhogal
Maria Gould
Ameesha Green
Paul Hindle

Indexers
Tejal Soni
Priya Subramani

Graphics
Sheetal Aute
Ronak Dhruv
Valentina D'silva

Production Coordinator
Manu Joseph

Cover Work
Manu Joseph

About the Author

David B. Demyan is an instructional designer and screencast producer, busy delivering courses to organizations and developing e-learning materials for clients. Using Camtasia Studio since the early days of the product's release, he was hired by TechSmith to author the help system that accompanies the software. With each Camtasia Studio release, he gained expertise in using every feature. He has hosted training classes for industry, government, and educational organizations showing how to use Camtasia Studio to teach or inform.

Over the past 10 years, he has specialized in e-learning consultation. As the owner of Spectorial Corporation, he produces and guides others in the creation of software system e-learning materials using rapid development tools, such as Articulate Storyline, Camtasia, Captivate, and Audacity. The author's unique Show me, Try it, and Quiz me approach to teaching has earned high praise from both clients and the e-learning industry.

He offers hands-on training in using Camtasia Studio for e-learning, with this book as the primary text and additional resource. He can be reached at http://www.spectorial.com.

I gratefully acknowledge the expert help from the readers, reviewers, and editors, without whose assistance this book would not have been possible.

About the Reviewers

Jason R. Clemens retired from the United States Army and is now a training and e-learning/media specialist in Pueblo, Colorado, where he develops classroom and CBT courses in a specialized industrial field. His 18 years of training experience and involvement in education technology started during his time as an instructor in the Army.

While developing training for the Department of the Army, he found his passion for education technology. During this time, he was introduced to an early version of Camtasia Studio, and has spent the last decade expanding his experience creating screencasts for e-learning. Individually, over the past decade, he has tried to push the envelope of Camtasia Studio, by coming up with new methods and uses. To keep current with Camtasia Studio, he has consulted and spent many hours providing support on Camtasia Studio's online forums, freelanced with oDesk creating advertisement "How-to" videos for start-up companies, and provided one-on-one training for new users.

In December 2014, he will complete his Master's degree in Education Technology from Boise State University, Idaho.

When he is not working with Camtasia Studio and other technologies, he and his wife enjoy riding on their Harley and work to support veteran organizations and their causes.

Thanks to Pam Clemens, my beautiful wife, for all of her support. I would not be where I am today without you.

Richard M. Garetano is a training and development leader who has built successful training organizations for companies such as Racal Datacom, NextiraOne, and Cross Match Technologies. He has over 30 years of excellent management and people skills. He is a proven leader, communicator, problem solver, and analytical/strategic business partner. He is a person who loves challenges and strives to be the best and takes pride in his work.

He has the following development training skills:

- Instructor-led course development and technical and professional delivery
- Computer-based training development
- Training video development and production
- Interactive training development
- Web-based development and delivery
- Training needs analysis
- Test writing
- Training Internet and intranet site development
- Leadership skills
- Training organization development
- Biometrics: fingerprint, face, and iris

He is proficient in Windows operating systems such as 2000, XP, Vista, and Windows 7, and in applications such as Adobe FrameMaker, Word, PowerPoint, Visio, Excel, Adobe Acrobat, Photoshop, Jasc Print Shop Pro, WebEx, Go To Meeting, Camtasia, Captivate, Cornerstone Learning/Talent Management System, Test View, Articulate Storyline, and Adobe Captivate. He specializes in the development of training organizations, the development of technical products, sales, service, and professional training, Cross Match biometric product training development and delivery, development and production of professional and product training videos, learning and development, instructional design, facilitation, and project management.

His past work experience includes the following:

- Instructional Designer, TBC Corporation
- Training Video Development Contractor, Spectorial Corporation
- Learning and Development Manager, Cross Match Technologies
- Sr. Training Consultant, Cross Match Technologies

- Director of Training and Education, NextiraOne, LLC
- Technical Training Manager, Racal-Datacom
- Instructor / Sr. Training Analyst, Racal Milgo

He has written a number of product training guides for internal and customer training.

Sylvia Moessinger is a vocational teacher in healthcare, geriatric care special education, and computer science. She also works part-time for an e-learning institution that supports all universities in Rhineland Palatinate, Germany.

Since the late '80s, she has been working on computers and attends computer classes on a regular basis to keep up-to-date with new developments. In 2011, she finished her Master's degree in Online and Distance Education (MAODE) from the Open University, UK. She loves working with various web technologies such as HTML/ CSS, WordPress, Typo3, and so on. Camtasia has become a great tool to create videos for her students and other learners. She is a Moodle trainer and has experience in the development of Moodle courses. Lifelong learning is her motto, and she likes to connect with people around the world to learn more about e-learning, design, and other exciting topics. If you want to connect with her, follow her on Twitter at @Sylvia_I or visit her blog at http://sylviamoessinger.wordpress.com/. She also writes articles for http://moocnewsandreviews.com/.

Erika Smith is an instructional designer at TechSmith with over 12 years of experience as an instructor, designer, and developer. She has worked in a variety of industries, including Staffing and Recruitment, Utility, Software, and Technology. She has designed, developed, and implemented instructor-led training, asynchronous and synchronous e-learning, and blended courses. She has a Bachelor's degree in Engineering from Michigan State University, and a Master's degree in Instructional Design and Technology with a specialization in online course development from Walden University.

Travis Thurston is an instructional designer for the Center for Innovative Design and Instruction (CIDI) at Utah State University. At USU, he designs and redevelops online, f2f, and blended courses in Canvas LMS, consults with SMEs on campus to develop and deliver quality courseware, and finds practical solutions to various design and delivery challenges.

Recently, he gamified an introduction to HTML and CSS courses, and taught the online course as an adjunct faculty for the ITLS department at USU. He has reviewed books for Packt Publishing, including *Canvas LMS Course Design*, *Ryan John*, and has also had several articles published about the work done by the team at CIDI on websites such as eLearning Industry, eCampus News, and Edudemic.

He and his wife, Jenny, also spend time raising awareness about Type I Diabetes, and fundraising for the Juvenile Diabetes Research Foundation (JDRF) as co-race directors of the Crazy Pancreas 5k in Inkom, Idaho, and as co-committee chairs for the JDRF Walk to Cure Diabetes in Logan, Utah.

He began his career teaching high school history and physical education courses. Along with a BA in History Teaching and Physical Education/Coaching, he holds a Master of Educational Technology (M.E.T.) from Boise State University with a graduate certificate in online teaching.

www.PacktPub.com

Support files, eBooks, discount offers, and more

You might want to visit www.PacktPub.com for support files and downloads related to your book.

Did you know that Packt offers eBook versions of every book published, with PDF and ePub files available? You can upgrade to the eBook version at www.PacktPub.com and as a print book customer, you are entitled to a discount on the eBook copy. Get in touch with us at service@packtpub.com for more details.

At www.PacktPub.com, you can also read a collection of free technical articles, sign up for a range of free newsletters and receive exclusive discounts and offers on Packt books and eBooks.

http://PacktLib.PacktPub.com

Do you need instant solutions to your IT questions? PacktLib is Packt's online digital book library. Here, you can access, read and search across Packt's entire library of books.

Why subscribe?

- Fully searchable across every book published by Packt
- Copy and paste, print and bookmark content
- On demand and accessible via web browser

Free access for Packt account holders

If you have an account with Packt at www.PacktPub.com, you can use this to access PacktLib today and view nine entirely free books. Simply use your login credentials for immediate access.

Table of Contents

Preface

Video is an important trend in education as learners become more visually oriented and less willing to read textbooks. The generation of visual learners is already upon us.

You may be wondering how you will ever be able to reach this audience. For the past few decades, we have created classroom lectures, textbooks, and yes, even e-learning with limited visual content. What will happen if learners eventually expect all learning to be visual with little or no text? Will education morph from boring texts, slides, and lectures to glamorous Hollywood-style events?

That's not likely anytime soon, but you can certainly see evidence of the expectation. Video learning is all the rage right now. Everyone carries a video camera and everyone is an expert at making movies. Just tune in to YouTube and see for yourself. Why not extend those capabilities and skills to learning?

While it is not quite that simple yet, the drive to visual learning is firmly in place. New cameras and software technologies have made it easier than ever to break into the movie business. There is no reason at all to expect it won't happen in education.

That's where this book comes in. You have chosen the volume specifically designed to help you get up and running with Camtasia Studio to create e-learning videos. This versatile, powerful, and inexpensive tool can become your "classroom in a box." You will be amazed at the things you can accomplish quickly, easily, and without a huge software learning curve.

This book makes no attempt to teach you all of the many powerful features of Camtasia Studio. Instead, it focuses on those features that support the creation of professional e-learning videos that are ready to be uploaded on a website or learning management system.

If you were somehow able to see me working at my desk at the daily business of doing exactly what Camtasia Studio was designed to do, you would likely see the occasional quirk of a smile or hear a satisfied sigh of contentment. I really like doing this. It's a joy to get started each morning. Maybe I was smiling because I was able to accomplish some trick of transferring knowledge in record time, with high visibility and exceptional quality. Nothing else compares in the e-learning world to knowing you have the right tool for the job and you know how to use it.

Get ready to join me in the magic journey of gaining skills and knowledge creating fantastic e-learning videos that really work using Camtasia Studio.

What this book covers

Chapter 1, Getting Started with Course Development, begins to show you the possibilities of course creation with a goal of delivering those courses in video format. The focus in this chapter is helping you understand how the medium works in educating others. The importance of planning is discussed. Reading this chapter will enable you to get started in Camtasia Studio with a sound base of knowledge.

Chapter 2, Planning the Project, presents and describes the sample project plan. Like any e-learning project, planning is crucial to success. You'll learn about the many facets of the plan you've never considered before. Awareness of many things to consider when planning an e-learning video is vital to creating an effective and high-quality video.

Chapter 3, Creating the Script, describes how to create a script document that defines your e-learning video in the planning stage. You will learn what to include in the script and how to format it for easy use in production.

Chapter 4, Creating the Storyboard, explains why you need a storyboard and what to include. Steps to engage a review team and subject matter experts are explained. You will also learn about a shot list, a sort of visual "shopping list" of items to record and procure.

Chapter 5, Recording Basics, covers the specifics of using Camtasia Recorder. All of the technical aspects of recording on a computer, as well as the appropriate settings to use, are described. It includes step-by-step instructions to use Camtasia Recorder, as well as information about using Audacity, a freeware audio recorder. Using a virtual whiteboard and pen tablet is also described.

Chapter 6, Editing the Project, contains a comprehensive series of descriptions and Try it exercises when editing with Camtasia Studio for an e-learning audience. Use the timeline and editing features are described step by step. You will be introduced to a sample project using CuePrompter, which is provided with this book. The exercises will have you duplicating these results in well-defined steps. At the end of this chapter, you will have a project ready to produce and use.

Chapter 7, Quizzes and Interactions, describes two main types of video interactions possible with Camtasia Studio: action hotspots and quizzes. You will learn how to create clickable hotspots to allow your viewers to navigate within the video, how to include a quiz on the timeline, and how to make the production settings that will enable them.

Chapter 8, Deploying Your E-learning Video to the Web or LMS, describes the practical application of quiz interactions. Topics include capturing learners' actions, hosting your courses in an LMS, as well as using SCORM, Moodle, and other methods. We include steps to set the correct production options so your video can interface with web pages and learning management systems.

Appendix describes the sample Camtasia Studio project files, document samples, and templates. Instructions for downloading and expanding the samples are given. A list of references is included providing links to software and articles cited in the book, as well as resources for continuing education in the e-learning video.

What you need for this book

You will need to acquire the following software and items to take full advantage of the information in this book:

- Camtasia Studio: The Try it exercises in this book were done with version 8.4. A free trial version is available at http://www.techsmith.com/.

- Audacity (freeware) or other audio recording software is optional. Some of the Try it exercises feature use of Audacity, which is recommended. It is available at http://audacity.sourceforge.net/.

- Word processing software is needed. The samples and templates were created with Microsoft Word 2010. If you don't have that, the files can be opened and edited with freeware such as Open Office.

- A good microphone is highly recommended. The best option is a high-quality USB microphone, commonly available for less than US $100. Headset microphone combinations are not recommended.

- A video camcorder or webcam is optional. You will need one of these if live video will be included in your e-learning projects.

Who this book is for

If you want to educate others using video, this is the book for you. Teachers, designers, corporate learning staff members, and anyone interested in showing others how to do something will benefit from the expertise, knowledge, and skills gained in this book. Whether you are brand new to e-learning or you are a seasoned expert, you will be able to master the basics and advanced features of Camtasia Studio to create effective, attractive, and professional e-learning videos. In addition, you will gain an understanding of the unique medium of video and the role it plays in teaching. No previous knowledge of Camtasia Studio or video production is required.

Conventions

In this book, you will find a number of styles of text that distinguish between different kinds of information. Here are some examples of these styles and an explanation of their meaning.

Code words in text, database table names, folder names, filenames, file extensions, pathnames, dummy URLs, user input, and Twitter handles are shown as follows: "The Camtasia Studio project file features a unique file name extension: .CAMPROJ."

New terms and **important words** are shown in plain bold text. Words that you see on the screen, in menus or dialog boxes for example, appear in the text like this: "Set the **Fade in** and **Fade out** times to one second."

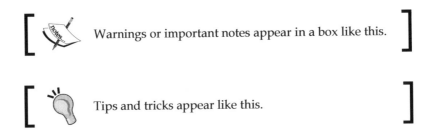

Warnings or important notes appear in a box like this.

Tips and tricks appear like this.

Reader feedback

Feedback from our readers is always welcome. Let us know what you think about this book—what you liked or may have disliked. Reader feedback is important for us to develop titles that you really get the most out of.

To send us general feedback, simply send an e-mail to feedback@packtpub.com, and mention the book title via the subject of your message.

If there is a topic that you have expertise in and you are interested in either writing or contributing to a book, see our author guide on www.packtpub.com/authors.

Customer support

Now that you are the proud owner of a Packt book, we have a number of things to help you to get the most from your purchase.

Downloading the documents and samples

You can download the example files for all Packt books you have purchased from your account at http://www.packtpub.com. If you purchased this book elsewhere, you can visit http://www.packtpub.com/support and register to have the files e-mailed directly to you.

Downloading the color images of this book

We also provide you a PDF file that has color images of the screenshots/diagrams used in this book. The color images will help you better understand the changes in the output. You can download this file from: https://www.packtpub.com/sites/default/files/downloads/8665OT_ColoredImages.pdf.

Errata

Although we have taken every care to ensure the accuracy of our content, mistakes do happen. If you find a mistake in one of our books—maybe a mistake in the text or the code—we would be grateful if you would report this to us. By doing so, you can save other readers from frustration and help us improve subsequent versions of this book. If you find any errata, please report them by visiting http://www.packtpub.com/submit-errata, selecting your book, clicking on the **errata submission form** link, and entering the details of your errata. Once your errata are verified, your submission will be accepted and the errata will be uploaded on our website, or added to any list of existing errata, under the Errata section of that title. Any existing errata can be viewed by selecting your title from http://www.packtpub.com/support.

Piracy

Piracy of copyright material on the Internet is an ongoing problem across all media. At Packt, we take the protection of our copyright and licenses very seriously. If you come across any illegal copies of our works, in any form, on the Internet, please provide us with the location address or website name immediately so that we can pursue a remedy.

Please contact us at copyright@packtpub.com with a link to the suspected pirated material.

We appreciate your help in protecting our authors, and our ability to bring you valuable content.

Questions

You can contact us at questions@packtpub.com if you are having a problem with any aspect of the book, and we will do our best to address it.

1

Getting Started with Course Development

In this chapter, we will answer some of the questions you must have had initially about Camtasia Studio®. The goal is to get you started with the right resources so that you can begin creating professional videos quickly. You will gain insights into how this unique tool can help you accomplish your e-learning video goals.

You have purchased Camtasia Studio or have downloaded the free evaluation, produced by TechSmith Corporation, and are anxious to start using it as the powerful teaching tool it has become. There are plenty of resources available to learn how to use the program and perhaps you have even taken a course or viewed the tutorials available at TechSmith's website (`http://www.techsmith.com/tutorial-camtasia-8.html`).

The power of video teaching

First, let's think a bit about the medium we are using. Video is a powerful way to teach. It enables all sorts of new ways to show exactly what you want your students to learn.

Years ago, it was adequate to simply videotape the teacher's lecture and give students access to the video and other resources such as a textbook or reference material. In business, videos were produced by the media department for the same purpose, educating personnel. Just by consuming the media, the students would theoretically learn the material and your teaching goals would be reached. While this approach was effective in some circumstances, especially in the "soft business skills" and academic categories, it does not do so well when teaching tasks or processes.

Also, those early attempts lacked interactive elements such as asking questions, presenting different scenarios, giving instructions, and even demonstrating an understanding of the material through knowledge assessments.

Today, video occupies a proven spot in the hierarchy of learning modalities when encompassed in a well-planned and executed e-learning program. This exemplifies the power of teaching complex subjects by showing you how to perform a task and then allowing the learner to demonstrate mastery. For example, you can point out the exact location of a switch on an appliance and describe how to use it very effectively with moving pictures and words. A video show-and-tell is perfect for describing how to use a computer program. Even classroom whiteboard teaching can benefit from the special effects available in today's e-learning environment.

The challenge is to think about how to best use these inherent advantages when planning your project. Begin by asking yourself the following questions:

- What type of learning am I creating?
- How can I best show learners what they need to know?
- How will the use of a video enhance the learning experience?

What does this chapter contain?

Now you are ready to start developing courses, right?

Well, if you want to produce high-quality courses, based on sound e-learning development methodologies, you will want to review a few more topics before starting. Perhaps you still have some additional unanswered questions.

The following are some of the questions you might have about things you will want to review:

- What are my goals for this project? What knowledge, information, or skill does the learner need to exhibit when done?
- What are the best techniques to use (slideshow, lecture, or desktop video)?
- Do I need an outline? In relation to my project, what is the outline and what does it look like?
- What about a storyboard or a script? Do I need these?
- How can I plan what to record and what steps to include in the instructions?
- How can I assemble the information and recorded material needed to create the project?
- How about some examples or a sample project? Would these help me get started?

You are in the right place. These topics and more are covered in this chapter.

By the end of this chapter, you will be aware of the steps required to plan an effective, high-quality new e-learning project when using Camtasia Studio. Then you will be prepared to learn more about these topics in the chapters that follow.

What are my e-learning project goals?

Whether in the business or academic worlds, perhaps you have taught students how to do things. This may have happened in a traditional classroom or informal face-to-face sessions. Or perhaps, you have written procedures for others in your organization to follow. Maybe you have some e-learning background already and just want to brush up on what you need to know before getting started. Whatever the situation, you know from experience that setting goals before starting will help your project stay on target.

The topic of goal-setting is discussed thoroughly in *Chapter 2, Planning the Project*. You will learn the specific components of a good plan, which includes everything up until you start recording. We will cover setting specific goals based on learner analysis, the components of a good plan, and creating an outline. You will understand how the outline is used throughout the project, how it is modified if necessary, and the use of some tips and shortcuts. Finally, the sample outline will be introduced and how to use it will be described.

Considering the desired outcomes when setting goals

So you have chosen to use video as a teaching tool for a reason, right? Perhaps you believe that you can reach your goals using video, maybe less expensively, more efficiently, or even more effectively. Now you are on the right track to setting goals realistically.

There are a number of additional reasons you might want to consider when using a video. To understand this better, ask yourself the following questions:

- What will be different for our learners or organization after they complete the program?
- Will it increase sales? Reduce training expenses?
- Reduce employee turnover?
- Increase productivity?
- Increase knowledge and opportunity?

Perhaps it will accomplish some combination of these factors.

With your goal or goals firmly in mind, determine the best path to accomplish them. If you were presenting the learning material in a classroom, you would have limited your options to a live lecture at the whiteboard while referring to the textbook. Using Camtasia Studio, you have a different set of powerful options.

Consider learner needs when setting goals

Many producers get bogged down on this part of goal setting. It seems daunting to attempt to discover what your learners need to know. Your project will benefit from spending some time thinking about and determining what they need before starting. This applies to video learning material developed using Camtasia Studio as well as other methods. We will cover this topic in detail in *Chapter 2, Planning the Project*.

What are the best techniques?

Let's assume you have decided to deliver your learning package using video. That's a good start, but you have some more thinking to do and decisions to make.

There are some options regarding delivery technique, which include the following:

- A recorded slideshow, where you create everything presentation-style using software such as Microsoft PowerPoint
- A recorded audio-visual lecture, perhaps incorporating a slide presentation
- A computer desktop recording, where you demonstrate how to operate a system, software package, or website
- Location video, where you make a movie of someone doing a task
- Animations or stock images and footage
- A whiteboard presentation, where you draw the information on a real or virtual whiteboard while recording video

In all cases, a vital learning aid is an audio recording with commentary about what is being shown on screen. While it is possible to have a mute video, or one with only music, as a standalone method, this will not be as effective instructionally.

All the delivery methods mentioned in the preceding list can be very effective. The important point is to make a decision about what methods you are going to use and think about how doing it this way will help reach your learning goals.

We will delve into the topic of delivery methods in various places in this book, including a wrap-up in *Chapter 8, Deploying Your E-learning Video to the Web or LMS*.

How can I assemble source materials?

At some early point in your project, the following questions will be on your mind:

- Where can I get the information I need?
- Where am I going to get the material to record?
- What about subject matter expertise?
- How will my learners know they are getting correct and authoritative information?

Gathering information

I know about Camtasia Studio, video e-learning, and building e-learning courses. However, if you ask me to create a training program on modern oil and gas exploration, I am going to need a lot of help. I'll go ask the experts and rely on their knowledge.

If you currently teach a subject and have developed material to share with students, you might already have the majority of the source material you need. Simply determine whether they are accurate, comprehensive, and up to date.

If you are the training lead working as part of a technical team, determine who on the team can act as **subject matter expert**, or **SME**. In fact, you might have more than one SME on your team, which is even better. Rely on these individuals to provide expertise for your training.

If you neither teach the subject nor are part of an existing team, you will have some special challenges. You will need to assemble a team or find other sources of authoritative information.

Gathering assets

Many projects rely on assets that exist outside the material you already have. For our purpose, assets are pictures, illustrations, audio files, and perhaps video files that will be incorporated into your e-learning project. Consider the following example: you have been teaching a course to a live audience about workplace safety. You have a set of "props" you use during this lesson—a heavy box to illustrate the proper lifting technique, a ladder to show how to climb on safely, and a fire extinguisher to demonstrate how to point it at the fire properly.

Having these learning-aid assets in hand before starting the live lesson is a valuable tool, allowing the learners to visualize proper safety techniques as you describe them. But also, ask yourself the following questions:

- Will the same assets work in an e-learning video based on the same subject?
- How will I be able to reproduce that live experience in a video?
- Will I be able to use pictures or illustrations in place of the live demonstrations?
- Where will I get these items?
- If they do not already belong to me or my company, how can I use them legally?

Similar to creating courses for face-to-face learning, as you begin planning and before you start recording an e-learning course, you will need to find or develop both the raw information you are going to teach and the additional assets you might need. This might include relying on your existing classroom material, interviewing team members to gain the information you need, doing independent research to find information. For assets, you might have to create or acquire additional resources that are appropriate for e-learning videos. We will explore all of these options in depth in *Chapter 2, Planning the Project*.

What is an outline?

In the case of an instructional video, the outline is the same as a learning plan or a classroom course outline. The purpose is to plan the topics to be covered in the proper sequence. As in any creative process, outlining your project before starting is an important step. It helps you organize your thoughts, always with the needs of the learner in mind. If something is important for the learner to know, it should be included in the proper sequence to avoid confusion or mistakes. If it is determined as not important, it should be left out or covered in another project.

OUTLINE
Setting screen size in Camtasia

1. Objectives
2. Explain resolution topics
3. Describe aspects of screen size
4. Show examples
   a. Record
   b. Edit
   c. Produce
5. Conclusion & wrap-up

For this section, we will consider the details of the outlining process in *Chapter 2, Planning the Project*, and the sample outline included in *Appendix*. A sample project is also included with this book. The subject of our sample project is *Using CuePrompter*.

What is a storyboard?

Now, let's consider some parts of the planning and recording process that are most often neglected. I believe they are vital to the success of your project. A storyboard allows you to draw up the audio, or vocal, content and visual parts of your "story". A good storyboard includes the script of the vocal recording, as well as a description or "stage directions" for the visual part of the recording.

TITLE: Setting Screen Size

AUDIO	VISUALS
Welcome to the Camtasia Studio tutorial, setting screen size.	Display title "Setting Screen Size in Camtasia Studio®" Setting Screen Size in Camtasia Studio*
In this tutorial, you will learn about setting the optimal screen size in recording, editing and final production	Display as mentioned, bullets over animated title scene: Setting Screen Size in Camtasia Studio* OBJECTIVES Optimal screen size for: • Recording • Editing • Production • Ensuring highest quality video delivery

A storyboard gives you a blueprint for your video and keeps you solidly on track with your outline and plan, hopefully focusing on learner needs. In its simplest form for a short project, a storyboard can be a drawing with lines and sticks on a notepad with the words to be spoken in a separate script. For a more comprehensive project, you will need to create a storyboard before you start recording and production. Used properly, a storyboard ensures that your project will be more focused and cohesive. Your learners will gain more understanding of the subject and will appreciate the logical organizational structure of your video.

A storyboard also affords you the opportunity to have your vision reviewed by others before you begin recording and production. If you have clients, other teachers, SMEs, or project team members who can act as reviewers, a storyboard gives them an opportunity to provide you with valuable feedback when changes can be made more easily than later in the project cycle.

In *Chapter 3, Creating the Script*, and *Chapter 4, Creating the Storyboard*, scripts and storyboards are explained in detail. You will also see references to the sample documents in *Appendix*.

What is a shot list?

The optional shot list helps you plan the video recording session. It is a terse, step-by-step guide that you can print or have on screen while you are recording. Your first impulse when clicking on that big red **Record** button may be to freeze. This is normal and can be easily overcome. Having a written list to remind you where to start and where to go next is a big help. In a few words, a shot list reminds you of the sequence of events you are going to record. This illustration shows a shot list for a video that describes logging on to a system and setting profile preferences:

SHOT LIST: Setting Screen Size

1. Double-click on desktop icon
2. Username=jdoe@domain.com
3. Password=pa55w0rd
4. Click on Login
5. Select Profile(upper right)
6. Choose Refresh drop-down=hourly
7. Choose Font Size drop-down=12

A shot list is especially important for video recordings. Whenever the video camera or screen recording software is turned on, you are going to want to know what comes up next. The shot list will put your mind at ease about this. It gives you the proper sequence to execute the list of tasks you are going to record.

This technique works well for a sequence of events that you need to keep in mind while recording. For other projects where the sequence of events is already defined or well understood, you might not need a shot list at all. For example, if your project is based on a deck of presentation slides, the sequence of events is already defined by the position of the individual slides. A shot list in this case would be redundant. The shot list is described in *Chapter 4, Creating the Storyboard* and a sample is included in *Appendix*.

The sample project

This book includes a sample project that you can use to follow along and see these principles in action. You will gain a better understanding of how the information in this book relates to a "real-world" e-learning project created using Camtasia Studio. Let's take a moment to consider this sample project, which you can examine more deeply at the appropriate times when referenced in this book.

> Review the sample project description included in *Appendix*. The sample Camtasia Studio project can be downloaded from your account at http://www.packtpub.com.

The subject of the sample project is one that will be useful for your own consumption: *Using CuePrompter*. CuePrompter is a web-based teleprompter which I find useful in my own general courses for Camtasia Studio users. The following are the elements included in the sample project and associated material in *Appendix*:

- **Project sample**: This contains a link to a Camtasia-zipped project file and instructions on downloading and using it. You will be able to use the sample as a starting place in developing your own projects.

- **Project plan and outline sample**: The project plan and outline for the sample project is provided for you to examine and use. A template is also included to be used as described in *Chapter 2, Planning the Project*.

- **Script sample**: This is the script for the sample project. A script template is also included so that you can use it as described in *Chapter 3, Creating the Script*.

- **Storyboard sample**: This is the storyboard for the sample project with commentary about the format of the document. A script template is also included so you can use it as described in *Chapter 4, Creating the Storyboard*.

- **Shot list sample**: This is a sample of a shot list for the sample project with commentary about each entry and how it is used as described in *Chapter 4, Creating the Storyboard*.

- **Quiz sample**: This is a list of typical questions as they would exist in the sample project. The rationale and techniques being used are described to help you create similar quizzes as described in *Chapter 7, Quizzes and Interactions*.

The templates and samples

The Camtasia Studio templates and samples included with this book are a valuable resource for you to use in your own projects. I recommend you download them now so you will have them available for the exercises in later chapters. The sample project was created with Camtasia Studio. The sample project documents and templates are available both in the Microsoft Word format as well as on Google Docs.

> Review the template and sample descriptions included in *Appendix*. The samples and templates can be downloaded from your account at `http://www.packtpub.com`.

For those readers who have Microsoft Word, the sample documents and templates can be downloaded from the Packt Publishing website, as follows:

1. Download and store the file `Sample-Project-Using-CuePrompter.zip` on your desktop.

2. Expand the `.zip` file and move the document templates to your Microsoft Office `Templates` directory.

> To learn how to manage templates on your system, refer to `http://support.microsoft.com/kb/924460`.

3. When you create a new document, select the appropriate template. For example, in *Chapter 2, Planning the Project*, you will be using the `TEMPLATE-Project-Plan` document.

For those readers without Microsoft Word, the documents and templates are available in Google Docs format. Both types of documents can be opened and edited in Open Office applications. For instructions on using the Google Docs versions, refer to *Appendix*.

Summary

In this chapter, you got the opportunity to explore the answers to the questions that you must have had about using Camtasia Studio to produce e-learning videos. The scene is now set to learn about the planning, resources, techniques, and solutions you will be using in your journey. From here on, the book steps you through these topics and coaches you through the whole process of developing and delivering an e-learning video.

Camtasia Studio is a very robust and powerful tool to be used in creating e-learning videos. But just owning and using Camtasia Studio does not mean your e-learning videos will reflect the quality levels you hope to achieve. There is no guarantee inherent in the software that ensures that your learning objectives will be met. This chapter presented some of the other items to be considered such as posing questions you might have asked yourself and providing links to the resources in this book that will help you answer those questions. Going through the chapters that follow, you will learn the importance of sound planning and execution. You will have access to some well-crafted samples to guide you on your way.

The next chapters are about project planning, scripting, and storyboarding. After that, you will learn the basics of creating Camtasia recordings, editing the footage, adding quizzes and interactions, and finally, deploying your finished e-learning video to Web or learning management system. You will get ample opportunities to try out the techniques I describe using the samples provided with this book or your own projects.

Engage your imagination and enjoy the trip!

2
Planning the Project

In the previous chapter, we started with the basics of how learners will benefit from well-crafted e-learning videos. This chapter will consider the components of e-learning project planning and explain their role. Project planning is crucial for creating high-quality videos.

There are many ways to start your project. Some methods are clearly better than others. For better or worse, many published videos are recorded with nothing more than a computer, mobile phone, and an idea. While some of these videos are entertaining—mostly through sheer luck—many others are of little educational value. This is especially true of those educational videos that did not have the benefit of a well-written project plan. We have all witnessed videos purporting to teach us the fine points of using software only to discover that it was created by someone without any understanding of the subject or how to teach it. Viewers come away more confused than when they started.

Professional instructional designers and developers use project plans and pursue their activities in accordance with accepted educational standards. It is not within the scope of this book to provide a thorough study of instructional design. If you have not been exposed to instructional design principles, you are encouraged to study them on your own to learn the many aspects of planning and designing. See the references in the *References* section of the *Appendix*.

Even if you do not write your plans down, planning must occur. We will uncover some of the components of your plan and the importance of each one. Giving at least a token recognition to the planning of your project will help you organize your thoughts and consider all of the steps that go into a successful project. The more detailed and formal your plan, the better equipped you will be to start your work on the video. The following are some of the questions that will be answered in this chapter:

- What is a project plan and what will it accomplish?
- What subject or topic am I going to present?
- What is the scope of my coverage for that subject?
- What are the project goals and how do I define them?
- What resources will I need as the project progresses?
- What is a learner analysis and how do I conduct one?
- What is an outline? How much detail should I include?
- What if I need to make changes to the plan later?

By the end of this chapter, you will be able to create an effective e-learning project plan. Let's get started with the basics of planning.

What is a project plan?

The project plan includes your goals, resources needed, technical requirements, and an outline. It may also specify learning objectives if you know them. A good plan will make the execution of your project much easier and will help you avoid mistakes such as going down the wrong path and having to revise the project in the middle of production. These types of mistakes can cost you time and money and may result in a project that never reaches its potential.

Let's assume you have a specific reason for creating an e-learning video. The reason or reasons can be stated as goals you hope to accomplish by creating the project. You have some goals in mind, right? Think about those reasons and goals and then write them down in the plan. This will help you understand—and perhaps modify—the scope of your project. It is normal to include many extraneous goals in the project plan. Human nature is to try to accomplish everything at once. But thinking about and writing down all of the goals that have been rattling around in your brain will help you see the bigger picture; where your goals fit into the current project or perhaps overlap and necessitate multiple projects. In fact, it is not uncommon to plan an overall project and define your current one as a part of the whole.

For example, if you were creating a video tutorial on using Camtasia Studio, when you examine the subject you might decide you actually have three subprojects: using Camtasia Recorder, using the Studio Editor, and using the Camtasia Production Wizard. For each one, you would define the specific goals of your tutorial. This will help you later in defining the learning objectives.

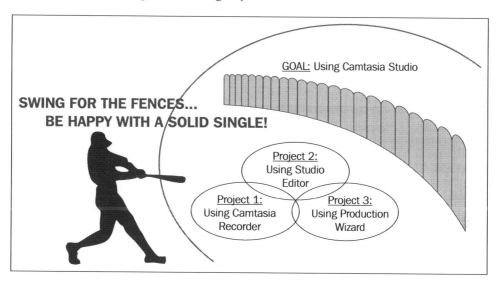

For an e-learning project, a project plan is a formal written document where information about the project is recorded and maintained. The main purposes of the plan are as follows:

- Identify the subject matter
- Define the scope of your project
- Set the goals and objectives of your project
- Identify the learners
- Specify resources needed to complete your project
- Create the subject or detailed outline of your project

Why is planning important?

One of the keys for creating an effective instructional video is planning. Your e-learning videos will be better organized, better focused, and more effective if they are planned appropriately. As an added benefit, whatever time you put into planning will be rewarded with fewer revisions and less cutting during production.

What will a plan accomplish?

If you buy into the concept that multiple eyes and brains on a project are beneficial, allowing others to review your plan and provide feedback is important. It is a good idea to consult others before starting the actual project creation. As an example, suppose you begin creating an e-learning video and plan to post it on the company intranet, along with a quiz at the end. After speaking with your IT department, you learn there is currently no way to keep track of who has taken the quiz on the intranet. A solution to this problem must be found since management wants to access that data. This issue could have easily been identified early and avoided by having the appropriate technical people review the plan and offer suggestions.

Selecting the subject

The subject and scope of your e-learning video are intertwined. While you may feel the subject and scope of coverage are self-evident, when you examine them, you might find they need to be refined. The subject and scope sections of the project plan allow you to refine your project.

Declaring a subject is as easy as stating, for example: "I am going to create an e-learning video about using Camtasia Studio." This can be defined in your plan by simply creating a subsection called `Subject` and stating it. The subject statement should be general.

Review information about the sample project plan included in *Appendix*. The sample project plan document and template can be downloaded from your account at `http://www.packtpub.com`.

See *Appendix* for links to Google Docs version of samples and templates.

For a real-life example of the `Subject` section of a project plan, refer to `SAMPLE-Project-Plan-Using-CuePrompter`.

Defining project scope

Scope can be defined as details about the project deliverables and your objectives. Scope is related to the subject because it defines the specifics of the subject. When considering the sample of a Camtasia Studio project, you might also consider the following types of questions when refining your scope:

- Will the training cover desktop recordings or presentation style, or both?
- Is it intended for commercial enterprise personnel or academic staff, or both?
- Will it include effects, transitions, callouts, and animations?
- How many advanced software features will be covered?
- What information should be excluded; that is, what is outside the scope?
- What constraints are understood to limit what the training can achieve?
- What assumptions can be made about the training and the learner at which it is aimed?
- Will there be exercises or quizzes? Will they be scored and how will that data be utilized?

Clearly, answering these questions within the scope statement of your plan will help you determine the details of your project, the real objectives, and what you hope to accomplish. For this, add a Scope subsection to your plan where these types of questions and others will be presented and answered.

For an example of the Scope section of a project plan, refer to SAMPLE-Project-Plan-Using-CuePrompter.

Setting project goals

As described in *Chapter 1, Getting Started with Course Development*, it is important to set your project goals before starting. This will keep your work on target and aimed at accomplishing those goals. In doing so, ensure your goal statements are specific enough and targeted to your learner's needs.

Be specific

You probably also know that your goals need to be detailed. It is probably not a good goal if it does not refer to something specific you want to accomplish educationally. These goals may turn into learning objectives later.

For example, it is probably not specific enough to write a goal such as: "Familiarize students with CuePrompter." A better set of goals would be:

- Describe the operation of the CuePrompter web application to a learner who is already familiar with using prompters

- Explain the steps required to copy text from a script and paste it into the prompter

- Explain the steps required to start, stop, speed up, and slow down the prompter scrolling

For an example of the `Goals` section of a project plan, refer to `SAMPLE-Project-Plan-Using-CuePrompter`.

Resources

The resources that are required can be anything, including information, equipment, software, images, sounds, bandwidth, or people, to name a few. They may be resources the e-learning developers require or ones the learners will require in order to view the finished learning program. In both the cases, they should be identified in the project plan.

What resources will I need?

Determining the resources required for your project involves considering the subject and scope. Once you have determined those, you will be able to identify the required resources. This aspect of your project plan is important. Having access to the proper resources is essential to fulfill the project plan and objectives. This does not imply that obtaining resources is necessarily expensive. There are ways to get access for little or no money. We'll discuss those options as they arise in the upcoming sections.

But you should try to avoid beginning work on your project only to discover you do not have everything you need to complete it. Identifying and avoiding situations like this early in the process is important to the success of the project.

The project team

An important resource is a project team. Yes, this may indeed be a team of one or two individuals who wear many hats. But, understanding who your project team is at the beginning of planning will help ensure the success of your e-learning video. During the project, some of the team members will be able to provide guidance on operational questions such as organizational goals, legal issues, and security. Others may be helpful in answering technical questions about your e-learning video delivery plans and some of them will review your progress and offer suggestions.

> If you are limited by not having access to an external project team, look for ways to supplement your own role. You can enlist the help of volunteers in some cases. Give them credit in the video for their contributions, whether they are paid to help you or not. A `Credits` section at the end of the video is a nice touch and encourages participation.

If the learning materials are already developed and approved, you may not need to assemble a team. However, if the material needs to be reviewed for the current e-learning project, you may need to get at least one other person involved. For many projects, a team is required. The more expert guidance you can obtain the better. And many team members will be flattered to serve on your project team, either formally or informally. It all depends on how you ask!

Assuming you have mastered the art of asking for assistance, you should again consider the scope of your project when determining whom to invite. Many organizations have the answers to these questions on the organizational chart. Choose individuals whose expertise and work responsibilities identify them as appropriate for your purposes.

The following is an example list of team members you could consider. Their roles may overlap.

- **Subject matter experts (SMEs)**: These are the people who know your chosen subject. Look to invite team members who might know something you do not or might have a different perspective on the subject.

- **Organizational reviewers**: These are the people who review and approve the material. This may be your supervisor, the head of the department, or others from whom you seek approval to publish the video.

- **Legal reviewers**: These are the people who can identify any issues affecting the legality of your materials, such as trademarks, copyrights, and compliance issues. Legal reviewers may include security experts who can judge whether the stated learner is authorized to view the materials you plan to release.

- **Academic reviewers**: These include the dean, department head, academic advisor, or admissions personnel. In the case of e-learning for educational institutions, you may also need academic peer reviews.

- **Editorial reviewers**: These are the people who review for typographical, grammar, and spelling errors. Look for someone with a sharp eye for detail.

- **Human resources (HR)**: This is the organization usually responsible for staff development. They may want to ensure your project fits with overall organizational development goals.

- **Media**: This role includes graphics, photography, or other e-learning developers, depending on your organizational structure.

- **Technical**: This role includes information technology and infrastructure experts. These folks can help you determine whether the existing software and systems will support your e-learning program.

- **Learners**: Consider asking members of your intended learner audience to preview your materials.

The following figure will show you the members of the team:

The review team

From your project team, you may be able to identify reviewers, another important project resource. Determine which team members will be designated as reviewers. The purpose of reviewing the plans, documents, and videos is to ensure appropriateness, relevance, and accuracy of the materials. The review team's job is to view these materials and provide feedback to you.

The review team is usually selected from the identified project team. Provide the review team access to your plan, outline, storyboard, and drafts of the videos as they are completed. Solicit their comments or feedback and request a quick response to keep your project moving. When you receive comments, it is a good idea to keep track of them and respond to the reviewers about how you addressed their contributions. And by all means, contact them personally for any questions or detailed requests you may have.

To allow you to trace back through the changes made in the project plan after initial publication, use a technique to track changes, such as using different text colors or the **Track Changes** feature in Word. This will allow you to spot changes at a glance, perhaps associating them with the reviewer who submitted them. Annotate changes so that you will remember the reasons they were made and who made them.

Software and systems

Technical resources are also important for success. There are two areas of software and systems to consider: the resources you will need to support the creation of your video e-learning project and the resources the learners will require when viewing the videos.

Ensure you have the correct workstation and operating system, the right authoring software including Camtasia Studio, graphics and audio editing software, and the correct microphone and headphones.

If you need to save money, look for good alternatives in the free and open source market, such as GIMP for graphics, Audacity for audio editing, and Open Office for the administrative requirements.

Ensure you have *enough* of everything to author your e-learning video successfully. Video editing generally requires a high-power computer, lots of memory, and a high-bandwidth network or Internet connection. Now is not the time to cut corners or make do with outdated equipment or software. Any special requirements may be identified in the project plan and requisitioned ahead of time.

While planning, think about what your learners will require to view the videos. Some of the questions to consider are as follows:

- What operating system and Internet browser will best serve the videos on their devices?

- Will they be able to access the e-learning on mobile devices?

- How will learners gain access to the videos? Is it via intranet, Internet, DVD, or LMS?

- Will they need headphones or speakers to hear the program?

This last point is interesting and may seem obvious. Your answer may be, "Of course they will have audio on the device they use! Who doesn't?" Once when I was performing a learner analysis of typical office workers in an organization, I asked about the workstations they would use to take the training. Many of them responded their workstations had no speakers or headphones and they were specifically forbidden to have them. Internet access was strictly controlled. Others responded that they worked in such a noisy area that speakers were nearly useless. In these cases, my plan proposed alternate ways for these learner segments to consume the videos, such as:

- Allow such workers temporary access to the training workstations in a quiet environment so that they can access the e-learning

- Include closed captions so that they can use the videos whether they can hear them or not

A related issue is providing a learning experience that is accessible to all. Have you considered what accommodations may be required for hearing-impaired and/or sight-impaired individuals? Will your video require closed captioning? Will it need to be published in multiple languages? The answers to these questions may require additional resources for your project.

For an example of the `Resources` section of a project plan, refer to `SAMPLE-Project-Plan-Using-CuePrompter`.

Learner analysis

Learner analysis is a task undertaken by the instructional designer or developer during the planning of an e-learning project. Completing learner analysis is important because you need to understand who your learners are so that you can communicate with them effectively. Also, you should realize that you may have more than one type of learner.

In the project plan, you may be very informal and cursory or you may be formal and detailed, depending on your project needs. In both cases, learner analysis should be addressed in the e-learning project plan.

Informal learner analysis

You won't need to do analysis when one has already been done or the learners and their needs are already so well understood that a separate analysis is not required. A good example of an informal e-learning analysis is the one conducted for an established public education class. The analysis of the students and their needs in the classroom has been taken care of by the governmental education department, local school boards, supervisors, and teachers. In such a case, it may be sufficient to say that *learner needs are established and will be addressed in this e-learning project.*

Formal learner analysis

For comparison, let's consider an example of when a formal learner analysis is required. A new software system is introduced to a diverse learner group of workers in a wide-spread business enterprise. One learner type will be tech-savvy, such as the developers and IT workers; they tend to work with computers all day and may even be familiar with the software already. Another learner type will be novice, such as the field tech work force. They may log in to computers infrequently or not at all, but will be required to use the new system. Addressing the needs of these differing types of learners will present some special challenges.

To conduct a formal learner analysis, you will need to interview people within the learner population or send them a questionnaire. Using a questionnaire is generally accepted today as a viable method to expedite and streamline the process. The types of questions you will be using are indicated in the upcoming sections.

Make sure you tailor your e-learning content to address the needs of the learners you have identified and analyzed. Be aware that some of your learners will be more advanced than others, as in our preceding example. While it may be tempting to aim the content at the least advanced of your learners, be aware that doing so may miss the advanced ones, and vice versa. Aim for a middle ground that keeps advanced learners engaged while meeting the minimum needs of your less advanced ones. Or split your subject into two courses: basic and advanced.

The following are some of the specific areas to consider. From this list, you can develop your own list of questions to ask your identified learners, either through a questionnaire or interviews.

- Who are your primary and secondary learners?
- What are their demographics? Consider age, gender, educational background, and culture.
- What is their reading or comprehension level?
- What is their knowledge and experience? How much do they already know?
- How much time will they be expected to devote to training?
- Do any of the learners have special needs, such as visual or auditory impairments?
- What is their preferred learning style? Will they relate well to a "show me" style of instruction?

Once you have determined the answers to these questions as they relate to your learner, present your findings in summary form in the project plan. Your findings will impact your thinking and planning in every other aspect of the project.

For an example of the `Learner Analysis` section of a project plan, refer to `SAMPLE-Project-Plan-Using-CuePrompter`.

The project outline

A project outline is almost always required in your project plan. Unless your video is very short and comprises only one topic or idea, an outline will help you organize your material in a logical way that will immediately make sense for your learners. After all, you would not want to tell them how to exit the software before you tell them how to log in, would you?

An outline does more than establish the sequence of events you will be covering. It will also identify gaps and help you to sort topics and subtopics appropriately. Think of it as a table of contents for your video categorizing main topics and minor topics beneath them.

In the case of an instructional video, the outline is the same as a learning plan a teacher would prepare for his or her academic class. The purpose is to plan the topics to be covered in the proper sequence. As in any creative process, outlining your project before starting is an important step. It helps you organize your thoughts, always with the needs of the viewer or learner in mind. If something is important for the learner to know, it should be included in the proper sequence to avoid confusion or mistakes. If it is determined to be not important, it should be left out or covered in another project.

We will discuss two main types of outlines: subject and detailed.

The subject outline

A subject outline is just that: a listing of topics or section titles. There are no details because you have either specified the details elsewhere or they are so thoroughly understood that the details are not necessary. A subject outline is roughly equivalent to a simple table of contents. A subject outline is useful if it is mainly for your own use and will not be reviewed by others. If you intend to distribute your outline for review, consider using a detailed outline.

The detailed outline

A detailed outline is one that presents the subject title and has a phrase or sentence of explanation. Detailed outlines are good for review purposes because they provide more information to your reviewers, allowing them to understand your intent for each section. The following figure shows you the difference between the subject and detailed outlines:

Subject Outline

1. Getting Started
   a) Goal setting
   b) Delivery methods
   c) Sample project
2. Planning
   a) Project plan
   b) Resources
   c) Audience analysis
3. Creating the Script
   a) What to include
   b) Objectives
   c) Organization

Detailed Outline

1. Getting Started – Quick introduction to the subject.
   a) Goal setting – what are my goals; what does the learner need to know.
   b) Delivery methods – what are the best methods to deliver the video.
   c) Sample project – present the sample project and explain what is included.

How much detail should I include?

There is a temptation when creating a detailed outline to just keep filling in details, effectively writing the storyboard. The detailed outline should obviously not contain that much detail. You should have enough detail in your outline so that reviewers can visualize what you intend to present. The detail should also facilitate creating the storyboard later.

If you know, *do* include notes in the outline about what the narration will say and what the visuals will be.

However, *don't* include actual narration, images, or screenshots. Leave those for the storyboard.

For an example of the `Subject Outline` section of a project plan, refer to `SAMPLE-Project-Plan-Using-CuePrompter`.

Using the project plan

Now you have completed the project plan. Other than distributing it to your project team for feedback, what is its purpose? One of the functions of a well-crafted project plan is that it can act as a source document for the script and storyboard, yet to be developed. To keep everything in the proper order, you can base the script and storyboard directly on the contents of the outline. These steps will be fully described in *Chapter 3, Creating the Script* and *Chapter 4, Creating the Storyboard*.

Modifying the project plan

Another possible function for a project plan is as a record of changes as they occur. Modify the plan as your project changes. This will help you keep all aspects of the actual production headed in the right direction as your project moves toward completion. The project plan should be considered a *living document*.

To make it easy to keep track of changes, add version numbers to the project plan filename such as `Project-Plan-Using-CuePrompter-v3`.

Try it – create a project plan

Now you have descriptions of every part of an effective e-learning project plan. You can try it yourself with your own project and use the plan in the latter exercises in this book. Doing it this way will shorten your project planning time considerably and result in a complete plan that will be easy to follow:

1. If you have not already downloaded the samples, do so now.

2. Open Microsoft Word and select the `TEMPLATE-Project-Plan` document.

> You can also open the sample project plan document, `SAMPLE-Project-Plan-Using-CuePrompter` and use it to follow along in creating your own project plan.
>
> See *Appendix* for links to Google Docs version of samples and templates.

3. Add the project plan sections for your own project, being as thorough as possible.

4. When done, save your new project plan with a unique filename. I recommend that you set up a project folder to hold all project-related files.

If your project plan is not perfect or complete, just save it and add information to it as it becomes available. As I pointed out earlier, the plan is intended to be a living document, modified as the project matures.

Summary

In this chapter, you learned the importance of project planning and outlining. You have reviewed some of the components of a good project plan and have seen examples of how a project plan is put together.

Producing a high quality e-learning video starts with a good plan. Without one, your video can wander and lose focus for learners. Worse, it could fail to meet the objectives you have in mind for the project. How will you know whether your course has met objectives if you haven't formalized them in a plan? How will you know if the training covers everything when you don't have a good outline of topics to cover? It is always best to start with a project plan appropriate to the subject and scope of your video.

Now, let's move on to the next topics, which include how to create a script or storyboard for your project. In the next chapters, you will build scripting and storyboarding skills based on the planning techniques you learned in this chapter.

3
Creating the Script

In the previous chapter, the topic of project planning was discussed. Examples of how to create your own project plan for your e-learning video were shown. In this chapter, you will learn the basics of script writing. Many e-learning videos have a running commentary to accompany the visuals shown to the learner, which is a recommended approach. The combination of visual and auditory communication is an important reinforcement that helps the learner absorb the concepts being taught. After all, do you think a silent lecture, with just pictures, would be as effective as one in which the lecturer was vocal and pointing out the importance of what was being shown?

A **script** represents the words that will be spoken or viewed while the visuals are played for your learners. Those words can be either audible, that is, they are recorded with a microphone and recording software, or they can be visible, such as captioning or a visual transcript; or they can be both. In all cases, the words are effectively merged and synchronized with the visual story.

While scripting is not strictly required to create successful videos, creating a good and complete script is important. In this chapter, the following topics are covered:

- Do I really need a script and audio narration?
- How can I organize and write the script? Where do I start?
- What is the appropriate tone for the script?
- What should be included in the script?
- How is the script used in video production?

By the end of this chapter, you will understand the importance of an audio script and be able to create an effective one from your outline. You will also be ready to either merge the script with a storyboard—which will be covered in *Chapter 4, Creating the Storyboard*—or record your audio track and go right on to record the video as well. Now, let's consider whether you should make the decision to create a script and add audio.

Do I really need a script?

Some teachers, presenters, and screencasters are so accomplished at presenting their material that they feel comfortable working without a script. Using this method, the presenter simply records his or her own voice while recording the video. They may feel comfortable working from notes or an outline with just a few words to remind them what to cover. If you want to try this approach, by all means do. It does not work for me. The following illustration shows the components of a vocal recording session, including a microphone, headphones, a script document, and a computer to record the audio:

If you try to "wing it" through the script, you should be aware of the pitfalls. While you may save some time if you can record video and audio together, the finished product will seem less well organized and might even look and sound amateurish. You may find yourself rehearsing and rerecording more if you work without a script.

Using a script and recording the audio and video separately is just better in terms of achieving higher overall quality. The following are a few of those advantages:

- You will have a chance to refine your ideas much better if they are fully written.

- Reviewers will get a better opportunity to understand exactly what you intend to include in your project. They will be able to see all of your learning content.

- You have the option to send the script to a professional voice-over artist for recording.

 If you use this option, it is easy to find professionals on the Internet who are willing to bid on your voice-over projects. Use a service such as the one at http://www.voices.com/.

- After writing a script and recording it, you will have an accurate estimate of the length of your video. It will be defined by the length of the audio recording. This will be valuable in determining where to add and where to cut.

- It will be easier to keep a track of revisions if you use a written script. When saving the files, include a version number in the filename such as Script-Using-CuePrompter-v3.

- It is easier to organize the learning content if it is written out fully so that you can judge the entirety of the written content.

How do I organize and write the script?

The last point in the list of advantages to using a script is that your video will be better organized. This is vitally important when you are creating an e-learning video. As you begin executing your project plan, it is easy to lose track of the organization that you created for the video in the outline. Assuming you have created a complete outline for your project, you have the starting point already for a high-quality script. One of the most important points of script writing and storyboarding is to follow the outline. That is exactly why you have one.

 For a sample of a working script, see the project file, SAMPLE-Script-Using-CuePrompter. Review information about the sample script in *Appendix*. The sample script document and template can be downloaded from your account at http://www.packtpub.com.
See *Appendix* for links to a Google Docs version.

What is the appropriate tone?

Scripts that are meant to accompany e-learning videos have a certain tone to them. You may have noticed that the narrator in e-learning video often has an authoritative, warm, friendly, and conversational tone exuding patience and a helpful attitude. These are important qualities for the sound in your e-learning video.

Teaching today is much more effective if it is positive, encouraging, and even rewarding. The tone you set in your audio script should be like that. Avoid a condescending, superior, or "I know something and you don't know" tone.

The following are some examples of good, positive statements with a conversational and friendly tone:

- Now, let's take a look at the main features in Camtasia Studio.
- You will be able to build really impressive and professional videos if you follow these best practices.
- How will you know when you have completed the exercise? You will see the **Congratulations, you have created your first e-learning video** message.

Notice the generous use of the first person pronouns *you*, *your*, and *us*. This helps create a personal link between the narrator or instructor and the learner. Don't be shy about addressing your learners directly this way or including brief, relevant stories from your own experience to enrich the e-learning video content.

 If you need help in delivering the appropriate tone in the audio narration, consider using a professional voice-over artist. Direct your vocal talent to use the tone you are seeking. Then select your vocal talent by the sound of their voice and appropriateness of tone.

What is included in the script?

In many ways, your video will tell a story. And like any good story, it will have some sort of build-up or **introduction**, a body or the **e-learning content**, and a **conclusion**.

The introduction will present a very brief overview statement and objectives for the video. Your e-learning content section will contain instructions or other course content. And the conclusion will provide a brief wrap-up and repetition of how the stated objectives were addressed.

For many of your projects, you will also need commentary or annotations throughout your script. These are directions to the voice-over artist to help create an error-free audio recording.

If you are following along, refer to the sample script,
`SAMPLE-Script-Using-CuePrompter`.

Commentary and directions

Like a play script or screenplay, you should include helpful hints for yourself or whoever will record the script. They are not to be read aloud. The commentary and directions placed throughout the script will help ensure an error-free audio recording with minimal editing or rerecording. Use a different color, such as **red**, to indicate to the voice-over artist that the commentary is not to be read aloud.

This section may include notes or instructions about any aspect of the audible portion of your program.

The comments can specify the background music to be used as well as how it is faded up and back down at the beginning. You might include instructions about pacing or pausing between each sentence. You could also put in global instructions, or notes about tone of voice, accent, or other special instructions to the person reading and recording the script.

The Introduction section

The first part of a good audio script is an introduction. You can place any type of introductory comments in the introduction as you see fit, but you should at least have an **overview** and **objectives**. The sample script has a placeholder for the Introduction section. The following illustration depicts the information typically included in the introduction:

The Overview subsection

The Overview subsection of the script sets the scene for your learners. You want to tell them the subject you will be covering and any special information or limitations they should know about.

The overview should be very brief. It serves as a quick orientation for viewers to let them know that they are in the right place. For example, the first paragraph could be a welcome statement.

The Objectives subsection

The Objectives subsection of your script is where you tell them what you're going to teach them. Use the objectives to provide an accurate outline of what you expect your viewers to learn. This sets expectations right up front and gives learners a way to measure their own expectations and eventual success.

> Bloom's Taxonomy formulates a regimen of setting learning objectives. If you are unfamiliar with this field of study, start by reviewing the information at Wikipedia, which has been curated and updated: `http://en.wikipedia.org/wiki/Bloom's_taxonomy`.

While strict adherence to Bloom's Taxonomy is not considered a requirement by all video e-learning creators, knowing the technique and terminology will give you some good information to help create your own objectives.

Try it – writing the introduction

Now, consider what you would include in your own introduction. In the Overview section, referencing the title of your video while it displays on the screen is a good technique. The rest is optional, depending on your content.

How would you write the Objectives subsection for your project? Review the ones included in the sample script and try your own. Use your outline to select those key topics that will become the objectives. And always consider the important concepts or procedures you want the learner to know at the end of their training.

Remember in *Chapter 2, Planning the Project*, where we discussed that the (project) goals may turn into learning objectives later? Now is the time to go back to the `Project Plan` document, review your overall goals, and reword them into very specific, action-oriented learning objectives.

The e-learning content section

This part of your script expands on what you have set forth in the outline and objectives. This is the teaching part of your e-learning video. The following illustration depicts the information typically included in the learning content section:

The content section often covers an academic subject or a business process. In the case of a process, the content comprises step-by-step instructions on how to accomplish a task or group of tasks. This section can also contain lecture material, especially if the e-learning video is for learners to comprehend new concepts.

For step-by-step instructions, be thorough and test the process you are teaching. Forgetting to include critical steps is a common failure in spoken instructions. If you expect the learner to perform the steps accurately, it is not enough just to *show* them. You must also mention it in the narration.

The most important characteristic of good process writing is that a learner who does not have prior knowledge of the process is able to perform it without error. If you have done your homework in the learner analysis part of project planning, your process writing will already be well-targeted. However, if you are in doubt, test your process with such users.

Try it – adding content

In your own project, determine the type of learning content you are going to include. For lecture portions of your e-learning video, your script will be written like a documentary or audio book on an academic or business subject. While writing this portion of the script, consider the teaching technique you are going to use. Will it be like a slide presentation? Will you need to show complex formulae or computations? Will you show pictures to enhance the concepts? These decisions will impact the way the script is written.

The Conclusion section

This portion of your script restates the objectives in terms of what the viewer has learned. This is where you tell them what you taught them or provide a restatement of your e-learning objectives. It reinforces for the learner exactly what your intention was and it should ensure that you covered everything you intended. The following illustration depicts the information typically included in the conclusion section:

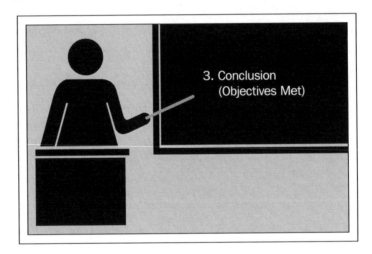

Your conclusion may lead into a quiz to assess learner knowledge after viewing the video. This is the learners' opportunity to prove they were paying attention and have mastered the material. In addition to being an evaluation tool, quizzes act as an additional learning opportunity. A quiz allows the learner to utilize what they are learning and continue to commit it to their skills or knowledge.

Try it – writing a conclusion

In your project, add a Conclusion section with a restatement of the objectives, worded similarly to the sample script. The emphasis in this section is on what was accomplished in the video.

If you are adding a quiz, base your quiz questions on the objectives and the subject matter covered in satisfying the objectives. Your learners will not appreciate it if you ask questions that were not covered. There is much more information on this subject in *Chapter 7, Quizzes and Interactions*.

 Pennsylvania State University has given effective quizzing a lot of thought, especially as applied to e-learning. See the relevant information at `http://ets.tlt.psu.edu/learningdesign/ effective_questions`.

How is the script used?

Your script represents the contents of the narrative of your e-learning video, the spoken words while the video plays. It may also be presented in visual form, as closed captioning or words printed on screen as the video plays. In either case, the narration must be added to the video in Camtasia Studio.

An approach that may work well is to record the audio separately while reading from the script. These topics are covered in detail in *Chapter 5, Recording Basics*.

Summary

In this chapter, we studied a sample script and discussed the important parts of creating a script for your e-learning video. As a teaching technique, using voice in addition to the visual images is important to reinforce concepts. Learners absorb the material much better when they hear the concepts and instructions presented the way a teacher in a classroom lecture would do so.

Creating a script or storyboard based on your project plan and outline will go a long way toward organizing your material in a logical way learners will understand. Consult the outline frequently while writing your script. Be willing to change both the outline and the script as your concepts solidify into a valid e-learning project plan.

Like any good story, a script includes an introduction, learning content, and conclusion. These three parts work together to set learner expectations, provide information, and reinforce what was learned.

The next chapter in this book is about creating a storyboard. Some e-learning producers may prefer to create the storyboard before the script, or to do so concurrently. These are good options, so choose the sequence that makes sense to you and your style of organization. Perhaps if you are more visually adept, you will prefer creating the visual part of the story before the narration. If you prefer scripting and then storyboarding, you have the advantage of knowing the textual story and its literal organization before developing the visual story.

So now let us move on to creating a storyboard, the next step in project planning. You will see how the visual parts of the story are developed based on the descriptions provided in the script.

4

Creating the Storyboard

In the previous chapter, you discovered how to use a script to spell out the audio portion of your e-learning video. In this chapter, you will discover the importance of creating a storyboard that merges the audio and visuals together. A good storyboard is just what it sounds like: a document, drawing, or combination of the two that defines the *story* you want to tell. It provides clear directions for the visual aspects of your e-learning video, alongside a script for the narration. In real terms, it is a series of pictures, sketches, drawings, or screenshots in one column with notes about what is happening at that time in the video. A second column shows the narrative words being spoken or shown in captions at the same time in the story.

If you have ever created a presentation with speaker notes, you are already familiar with how this works. In fact, there are no rules about how to physically construct your storyboard or what tools to use. Use any method that works for you and your reviewers. As long as it tells both the visual and narrative story, it should serve its purpose. You already have access to the one I recommend, a two-column template included with this book. A quick Internet search will turn up dozens of other good templates. The format you choose is not as important as the decision to actually use one.

Another step covered in this chapter is creating a shot list. This is a special document that specifies the actions to be recorded. As many recording sessions rely on the correct sequence of events, a shot list spells them out with enough detail the person recording the video can step through it and get the right footage.

Creating a comprehensive and detailed storyboard and a good shot list are important factors in the ultimate success of your project. The following are some of the topics covered in this chapter:

- Why do I need a storyboard? What does it accomplish?
- What should be included in the storyboard?

- Who reviews the storyboard?
- When can I start recording?
- What is a shot list? Do I need one?
- How do I create a shot list that will help me in making the video recording?
- How do I use the shot list while recording?

By the end of this chapter, you will be able to create an effective storyboard that will help ensure that the project accomplishes the goals set forth during project planning. As you will see, a storyboard gives you numerous advantages in video development. It will be available to external reviewers and subject matter experts so that you can gain feedback on your project. It also provides a valuable planning tool for you to develop how the audio and video work together to create a story.

You will also learn more about using a shot list to help you organize and manage the video recording process, ensuring a comprehensive, high-quality completed e-learning video.

Why do I need a storyboard?

Using a storyboard helps you and potentially other team members communicate important information about the e-learning video before and during its creation. There is a strange phenomenon at play in the creation of a video. What you think about, dream about, talk about, and plan does not always translate to a viable e-learning project without committing it to some form of reality. The storyboard helps you do that. It forces you to formalize and commit to the plans you have already created in the project plan, outline, and script. It allows you to bring all those parts together before you begin recording and producing. You will be amazed at how the simple step of creating a storyboard helps you develop your ideas in some very important ways that aid in accomplishing your learning objectives. You will see your ideas finally take concrete shape in a form that you can change as needed before committing them to a video.

The storyboard is usually reviewed by the SMEs and your client. As your vision begins to take form, so too will it begin to crystallize for the review team. If the reviewers take the time to visualize your project and synthesize your words and pictures, they will begin to understand your vision and objectives in ways they never considered before. It gives them an important opportunity to add to or modify the project before additional resources are expended in its creation. This is never as apparent as it is when consulting with a client. This usually brings together a team consisting of an outside instructional designer or project manager as a consultant and a client organization including their own trainers, managers, and other business stakeholders.

On a recent consulting assignment, my responsibilities included coaching client training staff in the proper creation of storyboards for hundreds of videos. Storyboarding was included as a project requirement for all of the good reasons already stated, but also for a very practical reason. The people doing the recording and production were organizationally and physically separate from the client personnel who would apply and administer the e-learning. We quickly realized that the storyboards would be a vital communication tool for consistency throughout the process of building the videos. The client was performing the traditional instructional design role and my consulting team was doing the recording and production. To fly without a plan and storyboard would risk misunderstanding the client's goals for the program, possibly putting the project in jeopardy. The constant flow of storyboards through creation, review, revision, recording, and production helped the team keep focus on all the vital details in the videos that would ensure success. Working without gaining the review team's buy-in and approval is a recipe for failure.

Using the script instead of a storyboard

For short videos and ones without a corporate budget, you may be able to accomplish what you need without creating a storyboard. For example, if you have no external reviewers, the utility of the storyboard is diminished. It is still a worthwhile effort for the benefits incurred in creation of the storyboard, but if no one is going to review it and you need to expedite your production times, you can certainly get by without one.

You can just use the narrative script instead. The words of the script may give you important clues about what to record for the visual stream. When I use this technique, I always highlight and annotate a printed copy of the script to remind myself what I intend to show for each part of the narrative. In this way, your script becomes an informal storyboard.

However, if you are working with reviewers, you will likely need a storyboard to communicate your ideas to them.

What to include in the storyboard?

The simple rule is to include everything you need to communicate your story effectively. It does not need to be fancy or take weeks to create. The number of reviewers you need for the storyboard is a smaller group compared to the reviewers for your finished e-learning video. The storyboard reviewers will want to monitor the concept as it takes shape. The storyboard is an excellent way to help them understand your content, both the visual portion and the audio.

Use the conventions, format, and a level of detail with which you are comfortable. I recommend including the following three types of information:

- Your narrative script
- Visual directions or cues
- Images, screenshots, or descriptions of what is visible on screen

We have seen how to create the script in *Chapter 3, Creating the Script*. The other two parts will be described in the following sections of the chapter.

Review information about the sample storyboard that is included in *Appendix*. The sample storyboard document and template can be downloaded from your account at `http://www.packtpub.com`.

For a sample of a storyboard, see the project file, `SAMPLE-Storyboard-Using CuePrompter`.

Follow the outline

Just as you followed the outline in creating the narrative script, you will need to do so in the storyboard as well. It is a good idea to identify the video title, overview, objectives, content sections, and conclusion. Each of these parts should be parallel to the ones in the outline you originally created. It is important that these two documents agree. If you need to make changes to the outline, do so at the same time you change the script or storyboard. It is not at all uncommon that as you begin to create the storyboard and fill in details, your outline and script will need changes. Let your review or project team know about any significant changes.

What goes where?

In your blank storyboard, you should have two columns: `Audio` and `Visuals`. The `Audio` portion of the storyboard defines the contents of the audio tracks in Camtasia Studio.

The `Visuals` portion of the storyboard defines the visual stream that appears in the video tracks and the preview window of Camtasia Studio.

The optional captions track (**CC**) on the timeline represents the visual presentation of the audio.

The Camtasia Studio timeline will be explained in more detail in *Chapter 6, Editing the Project.*

The following illustration shows the relationship between parts of the storyboard and the timeline you will be using:

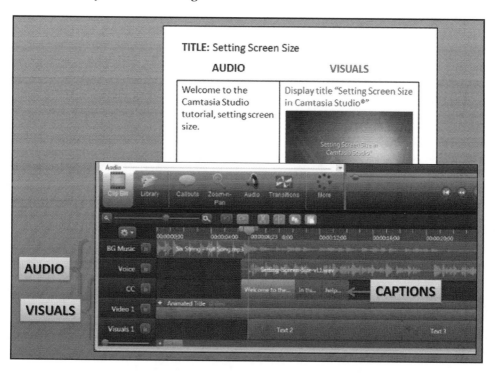

Incorporating the narration

This step is easy. As you review the audio script and create the visual definition in the storyboard, simply copy and paste the narration into the appropriate places on the storyboard in the `Audio` column. If you are creating the script and storyboard simultaneously, you've already accomplished this step.

Build the storyboard from the top downwards in sequence as it will appear on the timeline.

The video stage directions

In the visual side of the storyboard, as shown in the preceding illustration, include reminders in the text about how the visuals will appear. Some of the common directions you can use are the following ones, which are typical in screenwriting:

- **Cut to**: Rapid change from one scene to another
- **Display**: Show on screen to illustrate a point
- **Dissolve**: One scene melts or cross-fades into another
- **Fade in / Fade out**: Fade up from black (beginning) or down to black (ending)
- **Freeze**: Stop action or movement on screen
- **Insert** or **Superimpose**: Insert something into a scene, superimposed over the scene
- **Montage** or **Series**: A quick series of scenes
- **Pan**: Move from one section of a scene to another
- **Zoom in / Zoom out**: Increase or decrease magnification of a scene

There are other stage directions you can find yourself with a little research. Select the ones you find most useful in your projects. The most important point is to write something that will be clear to you and your reviewers.

The Visuals column

As you will see in the sample storyboard, the stage directions and visuals are placed in the Visuals column. Your visuals can be anything that shows what will be on screen. You can create sketches or drawings, images captured on a cell phone, or screenshots of your computer screen. The more scrutiny your storyboard will receive in the review stage, the more visual definition you should include. There should be enough detail to fully define the individual scenes of your video.

For example, let's say your storyboard has this direction: "Display the CuePrompter website home screen." To show this concept, I would take a screenshot of the CuePrompter home page. This is easy to do with screen capture software such as Snagit from TechSmith, the makers of Camtasia Studio. Then you can copy and paste the annotated image into the storyboard and resize it. You can do the same with images captured with a camera or a smartphone. For example, if you want to make a paper drawing, you can take a snapshot of that with your smartphone and import that into the document. Check out the TechSmith Fuse app available for iOS and Android smartphones to make this step quick and easy.

If it is impractical to include images, try using the graphics features of your document software to recreate a layout of what you want to show.

The important thing is to spend only as much time on the storyboard as you need to get a good idea of what will be shown and the words that will go with it.

Try it – creating a storyboard

Now you have an idea of how to create a storyboard and the samples to refer to. Give it a try yourself with your own project. Perform the following steps to create a storyboard:

1. If you have not already downloaded the samples, do so now.
2. Select the TEMPLATE-Storyboard template.

> You can also open the sample storyboard document, SAMPLE-Storyboard-Using-CuePrompter, and use it to follow along in creating your own storyboard.

3. Copy and paste portions of the audio script into the Audio column.
4. Create the visuals and add screen directions.
5. When done, save your new storyboard with a unique filename.
    I recommend that you set up a project folder to hold all project-related files.

The storyboard, like other project documents, is intended to be a living document that is modified as you make changes.

Reviewing the storyboard

One of the most important reviewers for your storyboard is you, the author. After creating your storyboard, wait overnight and review it with fresh eyes the next day. Do you think you can make a video using what you have created? Is it organized and coherent? Will it accomplish the learning objectives? Is it too detailed or not detailed enough?

When you are happy with your storyboard, distribute it to your review team. You can include those reviewers as discussed in *Chapter 2, Planning the Project*, the same team that reviewed your project plan. Consider adding someone outside the project team just to get different opinions. A good candidate for that role would be one of your prospective learners.

If you have been working with a learner or group of learners in other planning activities, ask them to review the storyboard. They will appreciate the opportunity and you get the benefit of them investing time and feeling ownership of the content. You should also include the paying client or a delegate if they are not already part of the project team.

Your storyboard should enable your reviewers to visualize your intentions clearly. After the review, include their feedback as appropriate.

Using the storyboard

After you have incorporated all feedback into the storyboard and have any necessary approvals, it's time to think about using it to record your video. Now is also the time to gather any other resources you might need, such as graphics, photos, stock video, or audio. If they are defined in the storyboard, you already have your "shopping list."

Before starting to record the video, consider another tool you can use: the **shot list**.

Creating a shot list

It is best to walk through the process or scene you are going to be recording as you take notes for the shot list. Get access to the resources you need, such as login information, Internet address, or access to the physical facility being recorded. Make sure the sequence is correct and you have all the information you need before starting. I usually write it on note paper and type the notes into the shot list document. The shot list document can be stored with other project files. It is a good idea to keep these files in case you need to reshoot the video later. For a sample of a shot list, see the project file, SAMPLE-Shot-List-Using-CuePrompter.

 Review information about the sample shot list included in *Appendix*. The sample shot list document and template can be downloaded from your account at http://www.packtpub.com.

The shot list does not need to be reviewed. It is for the use of the person doing the recording to ensure everything is covered.

Using a shot list when recording

The best way to use a shot list is to have it nearby when recording so that you can glance at it as a quick reminder of what to do next. Use any convenient way to display the list: print it and keep it near the monitor, open it on a tablet computer or second monitor, or simply move it off to the side somewhere you can still see it. Use it as a checklist as you go through the recording sequence.

Try it – creating a shot list

Now you know how to create and use a shot list. Consider using one for your own projects.

Open the shot list template provided with this book and enter the sequence of events to be recorded.

When done, save your shot list with a unique filename. Store it in the project folder with other project-related files. You may need it later if the video needs to be rerecorded.

Summary

In this chapter, you learned about the use of a storyboard and shot list to help you when recording your e-learning video. No matter what type of recording you are making, these tools make the job easier and allow others to review your plans. When the recording button is ready to go, you will be glad you are also ready to go. These tools will help you focus on making a good recording rather than on what to do next.

A storyboard allows you to define the story in precise terms and gives your reviewers a glimpse of what your finished product will be. It will also help you find gaps in the story or inconsistencies that would baffle learners if they were exposed to them.

Creating a shot list is a good way to keep your sequence of recording events firmly in mind when the recorder starts. It gives you a handy checklist to ensure you cover all of the steps in the correct sequence.

Now we are ready to move on to recording basics in the next chapter and topics on editing and producing the video after that. You will learn all of the steps required to create a high-quality e-learning video that meets the learning objectives. We will focus on the information you need to produce attractive and effective videos.

5
Recording Basics

We have covered the basics of planning for your e-learning video project in the first four chapters. Now the fun begins! It is time to put the planning principles to work and begin creating the actual video.

Today's process of recording is similar to the early days of Thomas Edison's invention of the phonograph cylinder and movie camera. Basically, you turn on a machine and point it at something to record, using either sound or light. These devices have undergone constant improvement and innovation for more than 100 years. It did not take long after the **personal computer (PC)** was invented to come up with easy ways to make recordings using the basic PC and Macintosh hardware with newly invented software.

There are two types of recordings you can make: audio and video. And there are numerous ways to make each type. We will discuss some of the ways recordings are made, but in this chapter we are going to concentrate on two ways: audio recordings using a microphone and video recordings using Camtasia Recorder.

I will also share some tips and tricks to use the recorders effectively.

The following are some of the specific topics we will cover in this chapter:

- What is required before you start recording?
- When is it best to record the audio script first?
- When is it best to record audio and video simultaneously?
- Setting up the screen and using the mouse properly while recording
- Using the script and shot list while recording

- Recording audio using Audacity
- Recording video using Camtasia Recorder
- Establishing the correct tone while recording audio
- Using a virtual whiteboard and pen tablet

By the end of this chapter, you will understand how to use all of the previously created planning resources in the process of recording both audio and video. You will also know how to record video from your computer screen and how to use a virtual whiteboard and pen tablet. We will focus on creating accurate and high-quality recordings, with an eye on how the quality of the recording can affect the overall effectiveness of your e-learning program.

Before recording

There are some things to think about, especially if you have never used your computer as a recording device. Today's computers are generally set up to make recordings, but not automatically. Just plugging in the microphone or starting Camtasia Recorder will get you started, but there is a bit more to it.

 This book covers only Windows-based PCs. Many of the programs and features mentioned also work on Apple Macintosh computers. Refer to the Windows system requirements at http://www.techsmith.com/ camtasia-system-requirements.html.

Use this section as a reminder of the things that you need to keep in mind to make audio and video recordings.

Microphone

You may already have a microphone but is it ready to make high quality recordings? The tiny microphone included with many laptop computers will record sound, but it is likely to be noisy and sound "distant." The audio recordings produced with an on-board microphone may sound "tinny," or like a bad phone connection.

You may have considered a headset microphone. These are convenient and easy-to-use. Just plug it in and you are ready to make recordings and listen to the playback. But these devices can be noisy. The microphone on the headset boom is usually no better than a laptop microphone.

Microphones are one area where you really do get what you pay for. It costs more to build a high-quality microphone than the cheap ones in laptops and headsets. The bad news is you have to pay more than a few dollars to get a good one. The good news is you can get a good USB microphone that won't bankrupt you. My advice is to set aside about US $100 for a good USB microphone. They are easy to use—just plug it in to an available USB port on your computer. Your operating system should load the correct drivers to make it work.

Consider also getting a **pop filter** and a microphone stand. The pop filter eliminates those annoying pops and hisses that can creep into your sound recordings when you form words with P, T, or S in them. The stand puts the microphone diaphragm up near your mouth where it can capture clear sound with a minimum of background noise. The following is an image of a setup that costs around US $150. Note the desk stand and pop filter.

You've seen fancy microphones used on television and in recording studios. You don't need to go that far, but you do need something better than a laptop microphone or headset microphone. If you have an opportunity, try out a few microphones before buying.

 The picture shows a microphone on a desk stand. This type of microphone is very sensitive and can pick up vibrations and fan noise. A boom-style microphone stand or isolation mount can help minimize these problems.

Camera (optional)

Camtasia Studio can incorporate and edit video footage from a camcorder. You can use any type of camera and import the clips into Camtasia Studio. In fact, if you have either a webcam or a smartphone with a video camera feature, you already have everything you need. The following are some camera options:

- **Video camcorder**: Most digital camcorders allow you to import footage into a computer. Depending on the format of the video files you import, you can further import the clips into Camtasia. If you need to convert the video files first, consider converting them to MPEG (MP4) format. Camtasia Studio imports the MPEG file type easily.

- **Webcam**: If you have a webcam attached to your computer, you may not need to import video clips. When you start Camtasia Recorder, you can use your webcam as a video capture device to record footage. This is especially useful if you are including a head shot of yourself in the video frame.

- **Smartphone**: Your phone may have a video camera and recording application. Camtasia Studio makes it very easy to import footage from your phone, which I will describe later.

Recording audio and video simultaneously

Many users wonder why they get poor results when they simply turn on Camtasia Recorder and provide a speaking commentary while recording the screen. While many people can do this effectively, others struggle and even find rehearsal and re-recording to be of little help.

It would be insufficient to say, "It depends on your personal preference." While this is true, the more pressing question is "What am I more comfortable doing?" or perhaps "Which method will enable me to create the best quality recordings given my preferences and abilities?"

This may require some introspection. People who have spent their careers speaking in front of groups, such as teachers and trainers, may be better suited to "winging it" while recording. Some e-learning authors have a low personal threshold for verbal errors or flubs. Nothing short of perfection will do. Those of us in that category are more at ease recording audio from a script and recording the video later. With practice, synchronizing the audio and video is not very difficult. We will cover this technique in *Chapter 6, Editing the Project*, when we discuss editing.

There is one area where the decision is taken out of your hands. If you are recording your own face while speaking, it is necessary to record both audio and video at the same time. This is because audio and video must be in sync; if not, viewers may notice your mouth moving out of sync with the audio they are hearing. This is very distracting and must be avoided. You also have the option of adding a screen recording or other video later. As long as your face recording audio and video are synchronized, you could be describing action or information that appears elsewhere on the screen.

Saving time by multitasking

If you are comfortable using this technique, you may be able to save a lot of editing time since you will not need to worry about synchronizing audio and video when editing. If there are minor flaws in the audio, such as pauses or using "uh" or "um," it may be easier to edit those out on the timeline later. We will go over that technique later. It may be worth trying simultaneous recording to see whether it works for you.

In this case, make sure your microphone is plugged in when you start Camtasia Recorder and set **Audio on**. There is much more information later in this chapter about using the recorder. Have a look at the following screenshot to go through the options available in the Camtasia Recorder:

After recording, if you are not happy with the results, don't be discouraged. Re-record it or try one of the other methods to record the audio and video separately.

Should I record audio first or video first?

The advantage of recording audio and video separately is that you can concentrate your efforts on each one individually. Trying to do everything at once, juggling the microphone, mouse, and storyboard all at the same time is difficult. If you find you are struggling with the simultaneous recording technique, try recording audio and video separately.

If you have followed along in the previous chapters, you have created a storyboard for your project specifying the audio and video to be recorded. Which one should you record first? Does it matter?

This is a matter of personal preference. Select the option that best suits your style.

If you record video first and then record audio, you have the advantage of seeing exactly what is being shown and then basing the audio (or revising your audio script) to match what is shown visually.

If you record the audio first and then record the video, the advantage is that you can play the audio while recording the visuals, assuming you have paced the audio appropriately. This can save editing time by having the actions and audio closely synced. If you use this option, consider slowing your audio recording pace to allow for visual actions being described to be completed when you record video later. You can always trim out any slow places later.

Using Camtasia Recorder

Camtasia Recorder allows you to define an area of your computer screen to make a movie. Every action you take on screen, such as moving the mouse, selecting options, or entering text, is recorded in real time. When done, you have a perfect replica of everything that occurred while the recorder was on. If you are recording audio, you can record every sound that enters the microphone and any sound the computer makes as well if you want them. If you want to exclude computer-generated sounds, you can turn them off in Camtasia Recorder using the **Audio** menu.

Explore the recorder options

Before recording, take a moment to explore some of the options. We will cover the most important ones in the following screenshot:

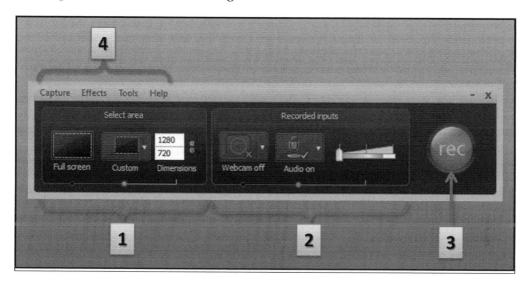

The options can be explained in detail as follows:

1. **Select area**: This part of the recording toolbar allows you to define the screen area you want to include in your recording. Make sure the area you select is appropriate for the recording you are making and will cover all of the options on screen that you are including in your video.

2. **Recorded inputs**: This part of the toolbar allows you to set up the webcam and audio inputs.

3. **Record button**: This one is simple; click on it once to record. Then it is replaced by some other toolbar selections to set up recording effects, delete the current recording, pause it, and stop recording.

4. **Menus**: The **Capture**, **Effects**, **Tools**, and **Help** menus contain features and options to operate the recorder.

 For more information about using these features, refer to the upcoming sections. You can also find video tutorials at http://www.techsmith.com/tutorial-camtasia-8.html.

Select the recording area

The best practice recommendation is to select a modest recording area with the 16:9 aspect ratio and maintain the same settings during editing and production. This will help keep the visual quality as high as possible throughout the process, resulting in a better-looking final production.

Camtasia Recorder and Studio describe recording and editing dimensions in terms of pixels and aspect ratio: **Widescreen (16:9)** and **Standard (4:3)**. These options are selectable in both products.

Pixels refer to the resolution of the recorded image. The resolution is usually stated as totals for the two dimensions. Accordingly, a screen that is 1600 x 900 pixels has by definition a widescreen aspect ratio of 16:9, and one that is 640 x 480 pixels has a standard aspect ratio of 4:3. This is shown in the following illustration:

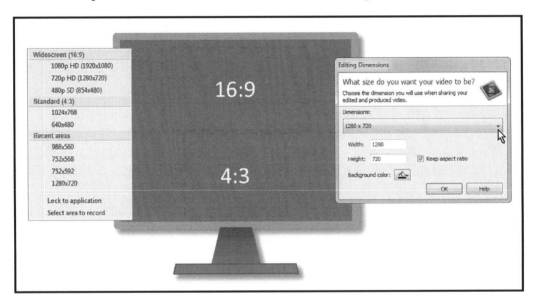

When is it acceptable to record a larger area? If you have not yet dealt with this question, you will. For example, imagine you are producing an e-learning video about a computer application, one that contains tabular data, such as a spreadsheet. Furthermore, imagine the table is so wide that it requires horizontal scrolling to access all of the columns. How would you successfully record such an application when it fills the whole screen and then some?

In some situations, you may need to record a larger area than you intend to produce. Let's say the only way to show all of the columns in the software application is to set the recording area to 1600 x 900 pixels. And you intend to produce a final video at 1280 x 720 pixels. In this case, while it is not optimal, the best compromise would be to record the larger area and then set either the editing size or the final production size to the smaller dimensions. There will be some minor distortion as the video is reduced to a smaller size, but using the zoom feature in Camtasia Studio will help alleviate that problem. We'll go over how to perform these steps in *Chapter 6, Editing the Project.*

Try it – screen recording

Now you are ready to record the screen using Camtasia Recorder.

For this Try it example, you will open and use the online application CuePrompter. The recording you make in this exercise will show you how to use this simple and effective application. You may even find it useful when reading your own scripts during audio recording.

The following steps show how to set up the recorder to capture a brief tutorial about using CuePrompter:

1. Open Camtasia Recorder but do not click on the **Rec** button yet.
2. Click on the down arrow next to **Custom** and select **1280x720**.
3. Open a browser and go to `http://www.cueprompter.com/`.

 CuePrompter is a narrow application. Reduce the window width so that the white textbox is located midway between the two sides of the window.

4. Open any script you have developed for an e-learning project.
5. Position the script next to or overlapping the browser window.

 You will be recording both the CuePrompter and the act of copying text from the document.

6. Position the two windows so that they are both within the recording area, the light-highlighted area on your screen. Your recording area should look like the following screenshot:

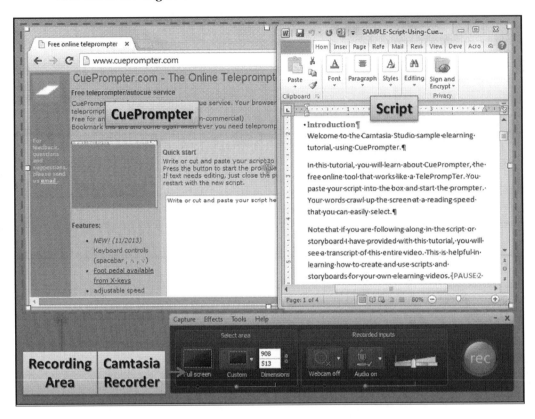

7. Select the document window so that the document is on top.
8. Click on the **Rec** button. The recording countdown begins, **3, 2, 1**.

> The recorder is operating when the **Duration** counter begins and the angles at the corners of the recording area flash white and green.

9. Highlight and copy any section of text on the document.
10. Click on the textbox (the white area in the middle).
11. Erase the words `Write or cut and paste your script here`.
12. Paste the text from the document into the CuePrompter textbox.

13. Click on **Start Prompter** at the bottom of the window. The prompter starts in a new window or tab.

14. Select the window or tab where the white-on-black text of the prompter window is located.

15. Press the Space bar to start the prompter.

16. Let the prompter autoscroll for a few seconds and then press the Space bar again to stop the prompter.

17. Press *F10* or click on the recorder **Stop** button.

18. Save your recording.

The recording is saved with a `.trec` filename extension. Make note of the filename and location. We will use this recording in later exercises to edit and produce your e-learning project.

 Store all project files in a folder named for your project. You will accumulate other files in this folder, such as audios, images, documents, and other videos. Double-clicking on the `.camrec`, `.trec`, or `.camproj` files will start Camtasia Studio while opening the selected file(s).

Using the mouse properly

The following are some points to remember when recording the screen with mouse cursor movements:

- While you were recording, did you move your mouse carefully?

- In the playback, does it seem to jump around too fast or move in directions that might confuse the viewer?

- Does it circle some object on screen as if to say "look at me!"

- Does your cursor speed up and slow down, seemingly without reason?

If you said "yes" to any of those questions, you will need to learn to discipline your mouse. It is really easy if you think it through before recording. You won't need to move the cursor at lightning speed or have it wander around in circles. The following are some mouse and cursor tips:

- Never use a touch pad or joystick instead of a mouse to move the cursor. Use a good mouse, moving slowly and deliberately in straight lines. There is no hurry!

- Do not circle the cursor around items you intend to mention or highlight. You can use callouts later while editing to provide a more effective highlighting effect.

- Pause over buttons or menus for a second before clicking.

- Minimize window scrolling as much as possible. If you must scroll the window, click on and hold steady over the scroll bar and move it slowly and deliberately.

- When moving the mouse, avoid unnecessary pauses if possible. Keep it moving at a steady rate.

- If you make a mistake, trace backwards to an area the cursor was previously, if possible. Then make the move again. You can edit out the mistake later.

- Consider setting up your cursor in **Control Panel** to a larger size or alternate color so it stands out.

Using the shot list

Before recording, review your shot list. These are the actions you will take while recording, so it pays to be familiar and rehearse from this list, if possible. Print it on paper or place it on another monitor so you can glance at it to review the steps quickly while recording.

Using Audacity to record audio

You can certainly use the standard audio operating system recorder or Camtasia Recorder to record a separate audio track, but the tip in this section will save you some time and aggravation.

 It is easy to use the freeware called Audacity to record audio from a microphone. It is available at http://audacity.sourceforge.net/.

Follow the instructions to download, install, and use Audacity. For a program that does not charge users a license fee, it is amazingly well-supported by a dedicated community of users and programmers. I have used the software for years. You can pay a lot more for a PC audio recorder, but you probably won't find a better one. Consider supporting this effort on the **Donate** tab at the download link.

Audacity tips

To save you some time and help you focus on the important features in Audacity, I have included some best practice tips, as follows:

- Plug in your microphone before starting Audacity. It won't be recognized if you plug in after starting.

- Record the audio that creates robust waveforms such as those in the illustration that follows. Adjust input levels to achieve these results.

- Use the **Noise Removal** feature (in the **Effect** menu) to get rid of hiss, fan noise, and hum. Select an area on the Audacity timeline that exhibits noise and then select **Get Noise Profile** by navigating to **Effect | Noise Removal**. Next, select the whole timeline and select **OK** by navigating to **Effect | Noise Removal**. Use a noise reduction of 15 dB or less to avoid digital quacking.

- Refer to Audacity **Help** and advice from the Internet community for more tips on using Audacity.

Using the correct tone while recording

It is important to read in a casual, informative tone so it does not sound like you are reading aloud from a script. This may take some practice and study on your part if you intend to produce your own voice-over content. It does not come naturally to most people. It takes preparation and practice to sound authoritative, friendly, and supportive. A pleasant-sounding, accurate audio narration is vital to communicating effectively.

The following are some tips to help you get there quickly:

- Read your script, but be ready to ad-lib or improvise to make it sound friendly and conversational.

- Sit or stand erect with your shoulders back to add depth and authority to your voice.

- Imagine you are speaking to a friend who is paying rapt attention to your presentation.

- Soften up your delivery and address the listener as "you." For example, "Now you should save your work so you don't lose it."

- Rehearse; if you sound stiff the first time through the reading, relax and try it again.

You may not be a professional broadcaster yet, but your spoken voice will begin to improve and sound better to your listeners. Keep at it until you like the sound, but recognize that even professionals are rarely happy with the sound of their own voice. If your speaking is clear, error-free, friendly, and knowledgeable, it will be a valuable asset in your e-learning projects.

Using the script

Print a paper copy of your script. Alternatively, if you have a large monitor or dual monitors, place the script in one area and the Audacity program in another area. Your screen may look like the following screenshot:

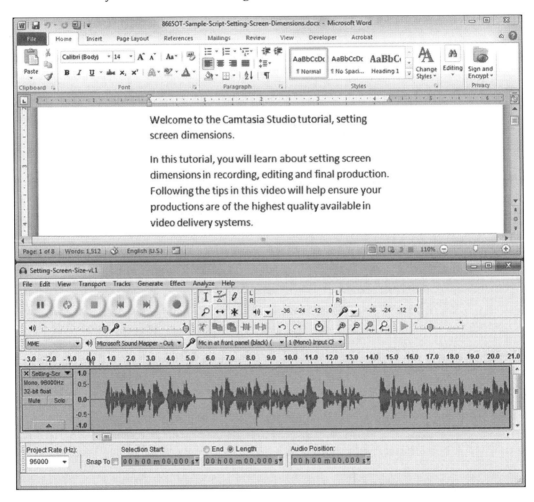

Try it – recording audio

The following steps show how to use Audacity to record your audio track:

1. Click on the red record button to start Audacity.

2. Begin speaking from the script and scroll down as needed.

 Scroll quietly so that the clicking sounds are not heard on the recording. I use a mouse scroll wheel to do this, which is very quiet. You can also use CuePrompter if that's easier for you.

3. Read at a normal pace.

 Don't worry if you make mistakes. Just pause briefly and go back to the beginning of the sentence to begin again.

4. When the recording is done, click on the red button again to stop recording.

5. You can listen to the audio file, highlight and select areas where mistakes occur, and press **Delete** to remove them.

6. When you are happy with the results, save the Audacity project file.

7. Go to **File | Export** to save your audio as a WAV file.

The WAV file will be imported later into Camtasia Studio to match up with the video recording you previously made. WAV is an uncompressed audio file format, so the files tend to be large, but since audio will be compressed during production in Camtasia, it is best to start with uncompressed audio.

Make note of the filename and location. Now you have an audio file to use in later Try it exercises.

 You have the option of using Audacity editing features to improve the audio before importing it into Camtasia Studio. I recommend using the Audacity **Noise Removal** feature to improve the sound because it works better than the noise filter in Camtasia.

Using a virtual whiteboard and pen tablet

If your e-learning includes material that should be presented on a whiteboard, you can record the process of writing on a virtual whiteboard on your computer screen.

There are some special requirements to record a virtual whiteboard session. You may need some additional software and hardware. I find it difficult to create handwriting using a standard mouse. When required in e-learning, I use a pen tablet attached to my computer like the one in the following image, a Wacom Intuos® which works well. I also use the stylus to make drawing easier than with a mouse.

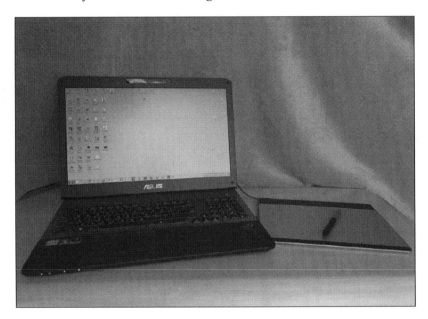

Try it – recording a whiteboard

If you intend to record the process of writing on a virtual whiteboard, it is best to use a pen tablet and drawing software. Once you have the hardware attached to the computer with the appropriate drivers loaded and a drawing application you are comfortable with, you can begin recording. Perform the following steps to record a whiteboard:

1. Start your drawing program.

 There are a number of whiteboard simulators available on the Internet. Search for the term `virtual whiteboard` to find some low-cost or free alternatives.

2. Open Camtasia Recorder but do not click on the **Rec** button yet.

3. Click on the down arrow next to **Custom** and select **1280x720**.

4. Position the drawing application window to completely fill the recording area.

5. Click on the **Rec** button. The recording countdown begins, **3**, **2**, **1**.

6. Use a drawing pen on your pen tablet to write the whiteboard content while recording.

7. Press *F10* or click on the **Stop** button in the recorder.

8. Save your recording.

If you want to include a virtual whiteboard session in your e-learning project, you can use this recording in later exercises to edit and produce your e-learning project.

Summary

In this chapter, you learned how to use Camtasia Recorder and some other applications to create your video and audio recordings.

Recording high-quality video is vitally important to the success of your e-learning project. Disorganized, error-filled, amateur videos will not suffice for e-learning. Such videos will not accomplish your goals or learning objectives because the learners will be distracted. It pays to take the time and effort to create high-quality recordings.

Start with a great screen recording, using smooth and deliberate cursor movements. A darting mouse that viewers have difficulty following visually on screen can lead to misunderstandings or distraction.

Good audio recordings, using a friendly, informative tone, will give your viewers important information they would not get otherwise. Addressing multiple sensors in the viewing audience will keep your learners engaged and receptive to the knowledge you are imparting.

Now we move on to editing and adding effects to your e-learning video in the next chapter. We will focus on those features of Camtasia Studio that can enhance the learning experience for your viewers.

6

Editing the Project

If you've been following along, you now have the planning document created that we covered in the earlier chapters. You also have a good video recording from Camtasia Recorder. You either have your audio within this file (if you recorded audio and video simultaneously) or you have a separate audio file (if you recorded audio at a different time than the video). In either case, you have the basic assets you need to begin editing your e-learning video project in Camtasia Studio.

The Camtasia Studio timeline is where all of your visual and audible elements come together. Using the timeline, you can layer audio, video, pictures, callouts, and even visual effects. With layering, you are in complete control of the timing—when things appear and fade, when voice or music occurs, and when content begins, ends, and segues from one part to the next. Using Camtasia features and the timeline, you can build your story, fulfilling the planning, learning objectives, and storyboard you have previously created. This is when the show begins to take shape and your vision becomes real.

We will cover the basics of creating a finished e-learning video using the editing features in Camtasia Studio. There is no attempt to be all-inclusive, as that would be unnecessary given the wealth of information available in the TechSmith tutorials and additionally would make this book too long to be helpful. The following are some of the specific topics we will cover in this chapter:

- Importing your recordings and visuals
- Placing assets on the timeline
- Choosing the correct editing dimensions
- Using the timeline
- Previewing your content
- Using the task tabs
- Laying out the visual aspects of the project

- Laying out the audio of your project
- Editing for good timing
- Enhancing the project with transitions, images, callouts, and zoom and pan effects
- Tips and tricks

By the end of this chapter, you will know how to accomplish an effective blending of audio and visuals using the timeline. You will also understand how to use the various visual effects available in Camtasia Studio and the benefits of each.

What is NLE?

You are entering the world of **non-linear editing** (**NLE**). Professional video editors have used NLE to create video shows for many years. This was traditionally very expensive then, requiring dedicated NLE computer workstations with high-end digitizing adapters, expensive editing software, and high resolution monitors. Today, many computers are capable of at least minor video and audio editing without special equipment or adapters. This has brought the art of video editing within reach of another kind of professional—the instructional designer.

A nonlinear editing system makes nondestructive changes to source materials. What does this mean? You perform edits that change imported video, audio, and pictures on the timeline. But the changes only apply to the output, which will be substantially different from the originals when you are done. The timeline and preview window are your **canvas** for defining those changes. So, NLE is a method of bringing change to the program without ruining your originals. There is no need to alter the original media if you can make a digital copy and change it electronically.

Throughout this chapter, I will remind you what is happening to your original footage, pictures, and sound tracks. It is important to keep your original assets stored where you can find them on the computer if you need them later.

Camtasia recordings

Before we get started, you need to be aware of some recent improvements in Camtasia Studio. The previous versions of Camtasia Recorder produced recordings that were only operable in the operating system in which they were created. The CAMREC file produced on a Windows computer would not work in Camtasia for Mac. In recent releases, interoperability between platforms was improved with the introduction of the TREC recording file. These are interchangeable between Windows and Mac computers.

To support older recordings, both types of files will work in the new version, except older files created in Windows will only work on Windows PC and older versions created on a Mac will only work on Macintosh.

Project samples

One of the best ways to get acquainted with Camtasia Studio is to look at existing Camtasia projects. There is a sample Camtasia project to which you have immediate access — the sample project included with this book.

You can review information about the sample project in the *Appendix*. The sample zipped Camtasia project files can be downloaded from your account at http://www.packtpub.com.

The sample project – Using CuePrompter

I have created a sample Camtasia project for you to accompany the exercises in this book: *Using CuePrompter*. When you are done with this chapter, if your timeline looks anything like the sample one, you did well. Open the project and review it by clicking on the **Play** button below the preview window. As it plays, watch the items pass by on the screen and on the timeline. You will begin to see relationships between what appears on the timeline and what you are seeing in the preview window. There is an illustration of the Camtasia Studio interface in the upcoming section of this chapter.

The upcoming sections describe building the sample Camtasia project. You can follow and perform the same actions yourself using the Try it exercises. At the end, you will have a production-ready set of files.

Importing media

When you have recorded audio and video to use in a project, your first step is to import those items into Camtasia Studio. Whenever you import assets into Camtasia, they reside first in the **Clip Bin** panel.

Keep in mind that assets imported to the timeline are copies of your originals. They are not modified in the editing process unless you take deliberate steps to do so. Even when you perform your edits and save your Camtasia project, the original files are unaffected.

The Clip Bin panel

Images, audio, and video clips to be used in your Camtasia Studio project must first be imported into the **Clip Bin** panel. Then they can be selected and dragged from there to the timeline.

For the following exercise, we will capture an image from the CuePrompter website, import it to the **Clip Bin** panel, and place it over the video at the appropriate spot in the timeline.

Importing methods

You can import media using a variety of methods. This allows you to bring in all the assets you need to build a video: audio files, videos, and pictures. The files can be on your hard drive, in Google Drive, or on a mobile device. This gives you tremendous variety to access items you need for your video.

Only compatible files are able to be imported. Nonsupported files are not displayed when attempting to import them and a red barred circle appears when drag-and-drop is attempted. Compatible files include:

- **Video**: CAMREC, TREC, AVI, MP4, MPG, MPEG, WMV, MOV (only one video and one audio track), and SWF (only files created by Jing or a previous version of Camtasia Studio)
- **Images**: BMP, GIF, JPG, and PNG
- **Audio**: WAV, MP3, and WMA
- **ZIP**: Import previously-zipped Camtasia project files

The following illustration shows the methods of importing media into Camtasia Studio, as well as locations of the major parts of the Camtasia interface:

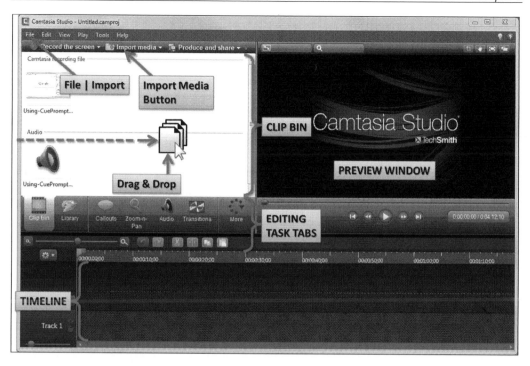

Using the File menu to import

Camtasia Studio has many options available under the **File** menu, including importing files. The following are the steps to import files:

1. In Camtasia Studio, click on the **File** menu.
2. To import one or more files from your hard drive, select **Import media...**.
3. To import from your Google account, select **Import from Google Drive...**.

Using the drag-and-drop method

Files can be dragged-and-dropped from a folder to the Camtasia Studio **Clip Bin** panel using the following steps:

1. Open a folder and select the files you want to import into Camtasia Studio.
2. Click-and-drag one or more files from the folder directly over the **Clip Bin** panel.
3. Drop them in the bin. Thumbnails or details about the file(s) are displayed in the **Clip Bin** panel.

Importing from mobile devices

This is a very handy way to import images, videos, or audio from your smartphone or tablet. This works with both Android and Apple iOS devices:

1. Install the Fuse app on your mobile device.

 For information on installing and using Fuse, see http://www.techsmith.com/fuse.html.

2. In Camtasia Studio, click on the **File** menu.
3. Select **Connect mobile device...**.
4. Follow the instructions that appear.

Importing a zipped project

You can import previously-zipped Camtasia Studio projects. A project can be compressed into a single ZIP file in Camtasia Studio by navigating to **File | Export project as zip...**. The sample downloadable Camtasia projects for this book are packaged this way. This process makes it easy to keep all of the files for a project together, perhaps to share with another user or for your own archiving purposes.

The reverse of this process is to import a Camtasia-created ZIP file. All of the original files—audio, video, library assets, and images—are opened and placed on the timeline with all of the original edits. This allows you to recreate the original project exactly as it was when created.

 When Camtasia Studio compresses files, all assets in the **Clip Bin** panel and timeline are included, regardless of where they are stored on your system. When a zipped file is imported, all of these assets are stored in a single folder.

Try it – importing zipped Camtasia files

Here's how to import Camtasia ZIP files. You can try the following steps using the sample file you downloaded to use with this book, Sample-Project-Using-CuePrompter.zip:

1. In Camtasia Studio, click on the **File** menu.
2. Select **Import zipped project...**.

3. In the **Zipped project file to import** box, click on the folder button to navigate to the sample project ZIP file.

4. In the **Import into project directory** box, click on the folder button to navigate to the folder where you want to store your unzipped files.

5. To open the Camtasia project after unzipping, make sure **Open project after import** is checked.

6. Click on **OK**. The sample project, *Using CuePrompter*, opens in Camtasia Studio.

   The **Import Zipped Project File** dialog box is shown in the following screenshot:

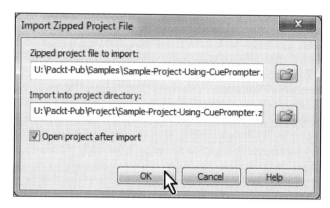

7. Preview the project to become familiar with it.

Try it – using the Import media button

Perhaps the quickest and easiest method to import files is to select the **Import media** button from the **Clip Bin** panel in Camtasia Studio. In this Try it exercise, you will start a new Camtasia project and import the recordings you made in the exercises of *Chapter 5, Recording Basics*. Use the following steps to do so:

1. Go to **File | New** to start a new project.

2. Click on the **Import media** button at the top of the **Clip Bin** panel.

3. On the **Open** dialog box, navigate to and select the files you previously recorded in Try it exercises. You should have at least one video recording and one audio file.

4. You can use *Ctrl* + click to select more than one file.

5. Click on **Open**. Thumbnails or details about the file(s) are displayed in the **Clip Bin** panel.

6. Save and name your new Camtasia project file.

If you are continuing with the exercises, keep this new project open for now. You will use this project throughout this chapter for Try it exercises.

Placing assets on the timeline

As mentioned earlier, Camtasia Studio is a nonlinear editor. Ironically, the process of placing items on the timeline in their correct order is very much linear in nature. Items are placed on the timeline in a linear order with an eye on the "clock," the time codes associated with these items. Timing will be very important in creating your e-learning video project. There is more about time codes in a later section.

Try it – placing files on the timeline

Earlier I stressed the importance of paying attention to recording, editing, and production dimensions. There is an easy way to set the correct dimensions for your e-learning video project at the outset. After placing a video on the timeline in a Camtasia project, I recommend setting editing dimensions at the same time. In this Try it exercise, you will place a video file on the timeline and set editing dimensions. Then you will place an audio file on the timeline.

Placing a video

This exercise illustrates how to place one of your recorded video files on the timeline. You can use the following steps to perform this exercise:

1. Start with your opened project file that you saved in a previous Try it exercise.

2. Select and drag your main video recording from the **Clip Bin** panel to the Camtasia Studio timeline.

3. Drop the video file on a blank track at the beginning of the timeline.

4. Repeat this process for any other videos you want to import.

5. Save your Camtasia Studio project file.

Setting editing dimensions

When placing the video on the timeline, Camtasia Studio automatically sets your editing dimensions to a size appropriate for the recorded dimensions. After placing and positioning the video on the timeline, you should check the editing dimensions and reset them if you want to produce a final video with different dimensions, using the following steps:

1. Click on the **Editing Dimensions** button above the preview window. The **Editing Dimensions** dialog box opens.

2. Click on the **Dimensions** dropdown and select your editing dimensions.

As a best practice, select **Original recording dimensions** for distortion-free editing and production. In the exercise and samples, this equates to 1280 x 720.

The **Editing Dimensions** dialog box is shown in the following screenshot:

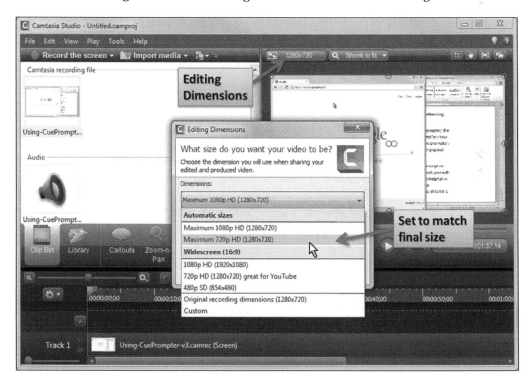

Make sure **Keep aspect ratio** is checked. The default background color may be changed to suit your needs.

3. Save your Camtasia Studio project file.

Placing audio assets on the timeline

This part of the exercise demonstrates how to move an audio file from the **Clip Bin** panel to the timeline. Perform the following steps with the Camtasia project you have saved from the previous Try it exercise. If your audio and video were recorded at the same time using Camtasia Recorder, or if your imported video includes audio, the following steps are not necessary:

1. Start with your opened project file, saved from a previous Try it exercise.

2. Select and drag your main audio file from the **Clip Bin** panel to the Camtasia Studio timeline.

3. Drop the audio file at the beginning of the timeline on a blank separate track from the video.

4. Repeat this process for any other audio files you want to import.

5. Save your Camtasia Studio project file.

Now that your video and audio are on the timeline, you are ready to add more assets or begin editing. First, let's learn a little more about how the timeline works. You will also learn about the tracks and how to use them.

Using the timeline

The Camtasia Studio timeline stretches horizontally, allowing you to build e-learning videos along a time continuum. It also stacks vertically so you can add layers to the auditory and visual composite.

 Timeline details are beyond the scope of this book. However, if you need to know more, there are good details about it at http://www.techsmith.com/tutorial-camtasia-8-timeline-in-depth.html.

Timeline and track description

There are several factors that make the editing timeline easy to use. Take a look at the following screenshot and the descriptions:

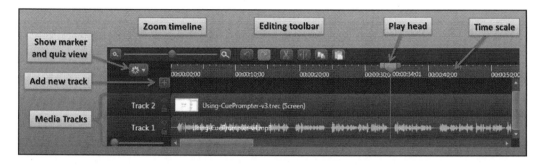

Media tracks

Media tracks are designed to contain your audio and visual assets. You place items on the timeline by dragging-and-dropping them there from the **Clip Bin** panel. There can be as many tracks as you need to contain layers of assets. The tracks can contain video, audio, images, and callouts. Markers, captions, and quizzes appear above the media tracks when enabled.

Adding a new track

Click on the plus sign to add a new track or simply drag an additional asset over the area where a new track would go.

 Visual assets on higher tracks visually overlay the ones on lower tracks. To overlay an image upon a video, for example, place the image on a higher track.

Timeline tracks have the following controls on the left-hand side:

- Click on the lock icon to lock or unlock a track; editing actions do not affect locked tracks
- Click on the eye icon to turn the track on or off

Zooming the timeline

Move the zoom slider ball left to zoom out the view of the timeline and right to zoom in. Zooming out shows more seconds of time and zooming in shows fewer seconds.

The editing toolbar

The editing toolbar has the basic editing commands for the timeline. You can cut, split, copy, paste, undo, and redo using the buttons on the toolbar.

The play head

The play head moves toward the right along the timeline as you play to preview your project. You can manually move the play head to any point on the timeline or drag to select an area for editing.

Use the moveable green **IN Point** and the red **OUT Point** to select and define the area, as shown in the following screenshot:

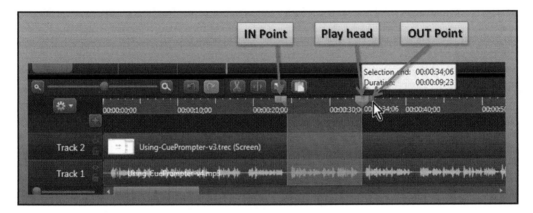

The time scale

The time scale shows a linear measure of time in frames, seconds, minutes, and hours, from the largest to the smallest increment.

 Frames on the timeline are arbitrarily set at one thirtieth of a second. There are 30 frames in each second. The play head is capable of moving or selecting one frame at a time, evident when you are fully zoomed in on the timeline.

The following image shows the increments in the time scale, which is located above the timeline. Note that **Frames** are separated from **Seconds** with a semicolon (;). The other time separators are colons (:).

The time code shown above the right-hand side of the timeline is an indication of the play head position. You will use each of these timeline tools in editing to create the perfect e-learning video.

Previewing the content

Camtasia Studio allows you to preview your assets, either from the **Clip Bin** panel or the timeline. To preview a clip from the **Clip Bin** panel, double-click on the file. It will play in the preview window.

The preview window

The upper-right portion of the Camtasia Studio interface is the preview window. The main area is a canvas where whatever you have on the timeline is displayed. Use the preview window to play back areas of the timeline to get an idea of what a sequence will look like in final production. You can also use this area to position assets and apply visual effects like animations. We will talk more about that later. The preview window is shown in the following screenshot:

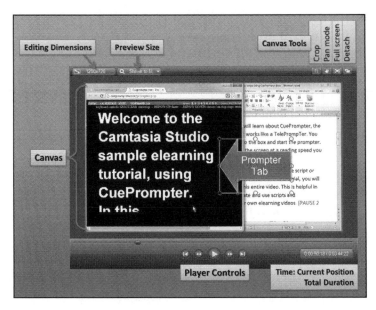

Canvas

The canvas area is where your video preview plays. You can position or alter your visual assets. In the illustration, note the handles around the prompter tab callout arrow. These handles allow you to rotate, resize, or reposition the asset.

Editing dimensions

Editing dimensions may be set by clicking on the **Editing Dimensions** button. Referring to the illustration, this control is located in the upper-left corner of the canvas.

The preview size

This dropdown (next to **Editing Dimensions**) allows you to select the zoom size of the preview in the canvas. Click on the down arrow to adjust the preview size.

Changing the zoom level in the preview window does not affect the size of your edited video. It is included so you can view details.

If your mouse has an active scroll wheel, positioning your cursor over the preview window and rotating the scroll wheel adjusts the preview size.

Canvas tools

Referring to the illustration, the first two tools allow you to crop or pan a visible asset. The remaining tools allow you to change the behavior of the preview window. Referring to the inset in the illustration provided in the *The preview window* section:

- Click on the Crop tool once to allow cropping and again to allow resizing. For details on this powerful tool, see the tutorial at http://www.techsmith. com/tutorial-camtasia-8-crop-mode.html.

- Click on the Pan tool to move the preview canvas within the preview window.

- You can also switch the preview to fullscreen and then press *Esc* to exit fullscreen.

- Detach the preview window from the editor—it will float wherever you place it on screen.

The time indicators

The time indicators in the lower-right section tell you where the play head is currently on the timeline and the total duration of your assets on the timeline.

Player controls

The preview window player controls work like most video players, with the **Play/ Pause** controls and controls to move back and forward.

Task tabs

You are now aware of the **Clip Bin**, timeline, and preview window. The main work in the Camtasia Studio editor is performed using the task tabs.

Referring to the following screenshot, the task tabs are located between the **Clip Bin** panel and the timeline. If all tabs are not visible, click on the **More** tab to see additional editing tasks:

Descriptions of selected tasks are included in the upcoming sections and exercises.

Laying out visuals

Keeping in mind the lessons about using the timeline features, you can begin to layer your assets and manipulate them to match your storyboard. It is not uncommon to spend the majority of your editing time working with visuals and matching them to the audio.

Adding a title

Working from left to right on the timeline, one of the first elements you will want to add is a title. A visible title is important for all e-learning videos to identify the subject you are teaching. You have probably never purchased a book without a title on the cover. Most learners would likewise not be inclined to open and view a video without a title to tell them the subject.

Titles appear as words on the screen for enough time to be comprehended. The words describe the content succinctly. In our sample, the title of the e-learning video is *Using CuePrompter*. These two words convey to the learner exactly what they can expect to see.

Using the Camtasia library

You can create a title manually, but there is an easier and better way to get professional-looking results. You can use the visual assets stored in the **library**.

The Camtasia Studio Library panel

The **Library** panel is where saved assets are stored. There are plenty of assets already stored there when you purchase Camtasia Studio. These include music, visual themes, callouts, and transitions. As you will see in the exercise, you can download new library assets from the TechSmith website. Or, you can create and store your own library assets, including video, images, and audio. You can select and save them in the library for future use. It's a great way to create a unique look-and-feel for your videos. It also contributes to consistency, which lets your learners know they are viewing a professional video.

Try it – adding a title

Camtasia Studio has features to make it easy to add a professional-looking title. If you have followed along in the previous chapters and this one, you have your first video on the timeline and you are ready to begin laying out the visual story.

In this exercise, you will drag-and-drop assets from the library to the timeline and position them as needed.

You will start with the project saved in the previous Try it exercises. Adding titles and other assets continues the process of building your e-learning video.

Save your project file often and after each Try it exercise.

Downloading a theme

To start this Try it exercise, you should have Camtasia Studio opened with your own customized exercise project. An audio clip and video clip are present in the **Clip Bin** panel and have been dragged to the timeline from the previous exercises. Perform this exercise using the following steps:

1. Open an Internet browser and navigate to `http://www.techsmith.com/camtasia-library-media.html`.
2. Select the **Themes** tab on this web page.
3. Scroll down about half way to the theme called **Light Maneuvers**.
4. Click on the **Download** link.
5. Save the downloaded file on your system where you can find it easily.

If you want to store it with other Camtasia assets, choose the `Media` folder located at `Documents\ Camtasia Studio`.

6. In Camtasia Studio, select the **Library** tab.
7. From a folder, drag the downloaded LIBZIP file over the opened **Library** panel. Drop it there.
8. When asked **Import zipped Library files?**, select **Yes**.

You can download as many of these free assets as you like. Check frequently for updates.

Using a title from the theme

The second part of this Try it exercise is selecting a title clip from the downloaded theme and placing it on the timeline. You can use the following steps to do so:

1. In Camtasia Studio, select the **Library** tab.
2. Scroll to the **Themes** section and click on the plus sign ⊞ next to **Theme – Light Maneuvers**.

3. Select and drag **Animated Title** to the timeline.

4. Drop the title at the beginning of the timeline. If there are no available tracks, drop it on the one with a plus sign button.

5. Now move the play head over the clip. Notice that the words **Enter Title Here** are visible for part of the clip.

Customizing the title

The third part of this Try it exercise is to customize the title clip to suit your e-learning video. These steps are recommended as a best practice. Feel free to modify the titles to suit your own purposes.

The animated title clip is grouped. This means there is more than one asset included in the title. You can tell it is grouped because it has a plus sign ⊞ at the leading edge. You can use the following steps to customize the title clip:

1. On the title clip, click on the plus sign to open the title group.

2. There are two parts: an MP4 video file and a text callout. Note the duration on the timeline, which is 30 seconds. Note also that the text part does not start for more than four seconds.

3. Refer to the following illustration. Position the cursor over the left edge of the text callout, and when it changes to a double arrow, click-and-drag left to begin showing the text at about one second.

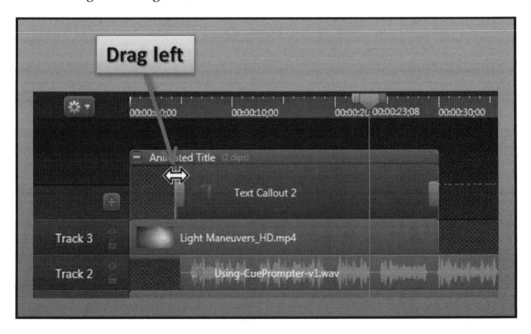

4. Double-click on the text callout, either on the timeline or in the preview window. The callout panel opens with **Enter Title Here** highlighted.

5. Change the callout to Using CuePrompter and set the size to 48 points.

6. On the preview window, stretch the side handles of the title so it all fits on one line. Move it right so it is over the lighter area of the background.

7. Click on the minus sign ⊟ in the upper-left corner of the title group to close it.

8. Select the right end of the title group and drag it left until the duration is about 8 seconds.

9. Preview the changes and save your work.

Your title should look like the following screenshot in the preview window:

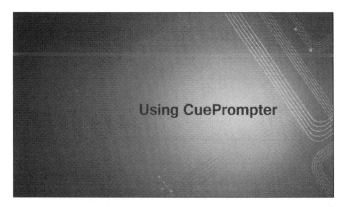

That completes this Try it exercise. You now know the basics of placing **Library** assets on the timeline and customizing them. Now, let's take a look at placing and customizing the audio.

Laying out the audio tracks

When you play through your video now in the preview window, you will see the title appear and your recorded audio will begin to play. The visual part of your e-learning video is beginning to take shape. Now, let's think about the audio tracks and what we might accomplish there.

Enhancing the experience

When you think about audio for an e-learning video, what thoughts occur to you? As a consumer of video content, you probably never gave much consideration to the parts that make up a program. If you go to movies, you can hardly ignore the audio. Surround-sound systems immerse you in a sensory experience.

In e-learning, audio can enhance the experience, but perhaps not in the same ways as entertainment. So, what does "enhancing the experience" mean?

In e-learning, our aim is to teach or inform. A well-constructed audio track in e-learning enhances the process the same way a teacher enhances the classroom experience with interesting comments, stories, facts, or perhaps other sounds. Conversely, if a noisy train is going by outside the schoolroom windows, some students' minds may wander. Don't forget that it is important to use audio in ways that do not distract the listener.

You have already created a script and audio track designed to enhance the learning experience. We will assume for now that it is error- and noise-free. Can it be further enhanced? Yes, with good timing, correct volume levels, and perhaps the addition of appropriate background music. That is the activity covered in the upcoming Try it section.

Try it – adding background music

This section will help you understand the basics of placing audio on the timeline and blending sounds from two separate tracks: narration and background music. We will use your previously-recorded narration audio and music downloaded from the TechSmith website to the Camtasia Studio library. Finally, we will make adjustments so the project starts with music while the video title displays, then the music fades as the vocal narration begins and the e-learning content starts to play.

Renaming and adding tracks

Before adding music to the timeline, it is a good idea to change the **Track 1** and **Track 2** labels to something more meaningful. This part of the Try it exercise shows you how to do that and also how to add a new track using the following steps:

1. Begin with your previously-saved Camtasia exercise project. It should look like the following screenshot:

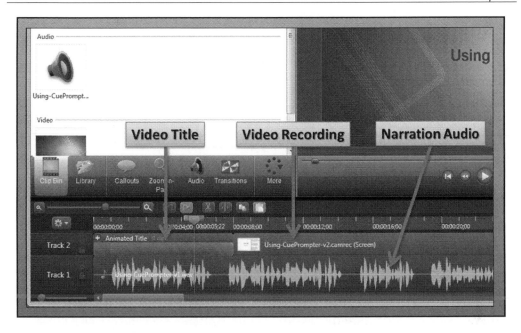

2. In the illustration, the narration audio is on **Track 1**. Right-click on the track label on the left-hand side.

3. Select **Rename track** from the menu.

4. Rename the track. For this exercise, call it Narration.

5. Right-click on the new Narration track label.

6. Select **Insert track below** from the menu. Another track should appear below the selected one.

7. Rename your new track as Music.

8. Adjust your view of the timeline so both audio tracks are visible.

One of the audio tracks is now called Narration and has your previously-created audio. The other audio track is called Music and is empty.

Downloading music

The following are the steps to follow if you want to download free music from the TechSmith website. You are licensed to use these royalty-free music assets with your Camtasia purchase:

1. Open an Internet browser and navigate to `http://www.techsmith.com/camtasia-library-media-music-tracks.html`.

2. Scroll down to the music file called **Six String**.

3. Click on the **Download** link.

4. Save the downloaded file on your system where you can find it easily.

> If you want to store it with other Camtasia assets, choose the `Media` folder located at `Documents\Camtasia Studio`.

5. In Camtasia Studio, select the **Library** tab.

6. From the folder, drag the downloaded LIBZIP file over the opened **Library** panel. Drop it there.

7. When asked **Import zipped Library files?**, select **Yes**.

> You can download as many of these free assets as you like. Check frequently for updates.

Adding background music

For this part of the exercise, we will load the **Six String** music from the Camtasia Studio library to the `Music` track using the following steps:

1. Select the **Library** tab, located below the **Clip Bin** panel.

2. Scroll to the music area and click on the plus sign ⊟ next to **Music – Six String**.

3. Select and drag **Full Song** to the timeline.

4. Drop the music at or near the beginning of the timeline on the `Music` track.

Your timeline should look like the following screenshot:

 The wave forms you see on the audio tracks represent sounds. Where the light gray shapes are largest are the loudest portions. Where the gray shapes are a narrow band, it represents low volume or silence. Use this as a visual guide to where sounds occur when playing.

Music timing and volume

In this part of the Try it exercise, you will be using the Camtasia Studio audio editor, accessible in the **Audio** task tab. Selecting this tab opens a panel that allows you to set volume levels, enable noise removal, create fade in or fade out, add editing points or keyframes, and create an area of silence. You can also multiselect clips to have your settings affect more than one.

In the exercise, we will adjust the timing and volume so it plays strong while the title is displayed, then drops in volume as the narration begins. Dropping the volume of one audio track so that another becomes more prominent is called **ducking**. Note that in the sample project, the Narration and Music tracks currently start about the same time, at the very beginning of the timeline. Perform the following steps to adjust the timing and volume:

1. Click on the audio file in the Narration track and drag it to the right so the recorded voice starts just after the title ends.

 Preview the project and listen to the audio. Note how the music plays for a few seconds and then the narration starts, but is almost overwhelmed by the music.

2. Click to select the **Six String** audio file in the `Music` track.

3. Select the **Audio** task tab, located below the **Clip Bin** panel. The audio editing panel opens and the green area on the audio track shows the current volume level, 100%.

4. Position the play head at about the 6 second mark on the timeline, just before the end of the title.

5. In the audio editing panel, click on **Add audio point**. A handle appears on the music track volume line.

6. Move the play head right about half a second and add another audio point. A second handle appears on the volume line.

7. Position your cursor over the volume segment of the `Music` track under the `Narration` audio after about 7 seconds.

8. Drag the volume level downward until the indicator shows about **20%**, as shown in the following screenshot:

9. Save your work.

Reviewing your results

Move the play head back to zero on the timeline and preview it again. You should first hear the drums, then the guitar begin to play at full volume, and then when the title disappears, the music ducks so you can hear the voice.

Now you know how to mix audio tracks on the timeline, ducking the music just before the voice starts. If your preview doesn't sound quite right, try listening to the *Using CuePrompter* sample project file and observe how this was done in the original. Modify your exercise project so that it does the same.

Locking the audio

Your audio is now done. The next part of this chapter describes making cuts and extending the video. Use the following steps to lock the audio.

 In the upcoming steps, if you do not lock the audio tracks before editing the video, you may inadvertently cut portions of the audio. The best way to prevent this is to lock the audio tracks.

1. Locate the lock symbols on the left end of the audio tracks.
2. Click on each one to lock the tracks. They should look like the following screenshot:

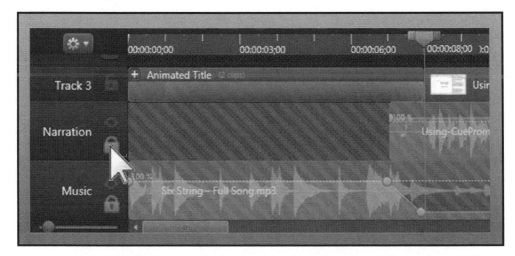

When the tracks are grayed out this way, any cuts made on the remaining tracks will not affect the audio. This concludes the Try it exercise for placing, modifying, and locking the audio part of your e-learning project.

Editing for timing

This part describes timing edits in your project. It includes techniques for adjusting the video and sometimes the audio so they are correctly synchronized. Basically, your narration should be timed to refer to actions as they appear on the screen. For example, when the audio says "click save," the video should show the cursor moving to and clicking the **Save** button on the screen. These timing edits can be made in the following three ways: cutting edits, extending frame edits, and adjusting the clip speed.

Try it – making cut edits

You have audio, video, and a title sequence on the timeline in your exercise project. If you recorded audio and video separately, after the title clip plays, you will notice that the audio/visual timing is off. For this exercise, we will use cutting edits to adjust timing so that events occur when they are described in the audio clip:

There are two types of cutting edits in Camtasia Studio, splits and cuts.

[Splits and cuts do not affect the clips in the **Clip Bin** panel. The **Clip Bin** panel keeps a copy of the original files.]

Splitting a clip

A **split** is a slice through a clip to create two separate clips. Each resulting portion can be moved independently. This is useful, for example, when you want to add time on an audio track. Split the audio clip into two and move the separate parts away from each other to insert a pause using the following steps:

1. In the sample project, unlock the `Narration` audio track.

2. Position the play head on the timeline where you want to make the split. In the illustration, the split occurs between sentences in the narration.

3. Click on the **Split** button ⬤ above the timeline (shown in the following screenshot) or tap the *S* key shortcut:

4. Click-and-drag the cut portion to the right to increase the gap and lengthen the time.

5. Relock the `Narration` audio track.

6. Preview the changes and save your work.

Cutting a clip

A cut is the act of removing portions of a clip or clips. When you make a cut, the portion before the cut is stitched to the portion after the cut. Cut edits are used when you just need to remove some time from a clip. It starts as a single clip and ends as a single clip, but with a portion removed. The cut portion is stored on your clipboard, and can be pasted elsewhere on the timeline if you wish.

 When the timeline area you select contains multiple tracks and clips, all unlocked clips are affected when you perform a cut.

Perform the following steps to cut a clip:

1. Lock the tracks you do not intend to cut. The lock icon should have a closed shackle.

2. Position the play head where you want the cut portion to start.

3. Click-and-drag the red end marker on the play head to the right to select a portion of the track. The example in the following screenshot demonstrates selecting a sentence of narration audio:

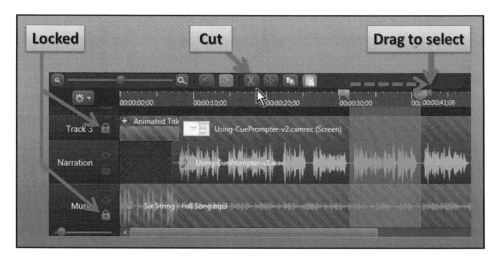

4. Listen to the selection to make sure you have the right audio selected.

5. Click on the **Cut** button (scissors) above the timeline. The selected portion of the clip is removed and the two remaining parts are "stitched" together. Locked tracks are unaffected.

 If you want to undo the cut, click on the **Undo** button (or press *Ctrl + Z*) twice to restore the clip.

6. Preview the changes and save your work.

Jump cuts

Both splits and cuts should be made judiciously, avoiding a **jump cut**. This is where the cut in a scene obviously jumps. Edits should be smooth and seamless so viewers do not notice them.

Extend Frame edits

An effective way to add time to a video clip is to use the Extend Frame feature. Since video clips are a series of static images, or frames, it seems logical that one of those frames could be stretched for a period of time to create a pause in the action and extend time. That is exactly what the Extend Frame feature does.

Try it – using Extend Frame

In reviewing the storyboard for the sample project, we know the first scene should be extended to allow the introduction and objectives to roll by. There should be no action in the first scene until the narration says, "…type (CuePrompter.com) in the address box." In the sample project, this occurs at about 1 minute and 20 seconds. At that point, our video clip should show the cursor going to the box and typing the address. On the current timeline, the action starts at about 10 seconds, so in the sample project, I added 1 minute and 10 seconds of no action. The following are the steps for using the Extend Frame feature:

1. If the video track is locked, click to unlock it. The lock icon should have an open shackle.

 There is no need to lock the audio tracks since Extend Frame does not affect them.

2. Select the video clip.

3. Move the play head to a position near the beginning of the video, just after the title clip ends. This should be an area where the cursor is not moving when played.

4. Navigate to **Edit | Extend frame...**. The **Duration** box opens showing the default extension of **1** second.

 The keyboard shortcut for Extend Frame is the *E* key.

5. Type the **Duration** value of the extension in the box. For the sample video project, that is approximately **70** seconds. Refer to the following screenshot:

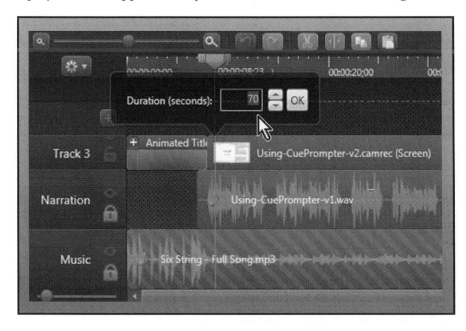

6. Click on **OK**. The video clip is extended the length of time you selected.

7. If the cursor movement to the address box does not occur at the correct time, right-click on the extended area of the clip to adjust it.

8. Preview the changes and save your work.

After adjustment, you should hear the narration say "...and the CuePrompter home page should appear" very close to when the recording shows it appearing. This concludes the Try it exercise for making Extend Frame edits.

Adjusting the clip speed

Your original clips have been recorded and saved in real time. This means that if the recorder was running for 30 seconds, the clip will be 30 seconds in duration. In Camtasia Studio, this is represented as a speed of 100 percent of the original clip speed. You can change the duration of a recorded clip just by adjusting the speed at which it plays. For example, if you increase the speed of a 30-second clip to 200 percent of the original, it will now move twice as fast and cover only 15 seconds. Conversely, if you decrease the speed to 50 percent of the original, it becomes slow and covers 60 seconds.

 This effect works well in video and not so well with audio clips, where changing the clip speed distorts the sound.

Try it – adjusting the clip speed

I find adjusting the clip speed useful to speed up an action that seems slow on the screen, such as typing text in a box. At my typing speed, watching individual letters appear one at a time is like watching paint dry. So thankfully for my viewers, I can adjust the clip speed in that area to keep things moving.

In the sample project, right after the area we extended in the previous exercise, the action shows the cursor going to the address box, highlighting the text already there, and then typing cueprompter.com. In my recording, the typing takes 6 seconds. To keep things moving along and incidentally to match the audio better, we will adjust that portion to 3 seconds. You will need to make two split edits and adjust the speed of the remaining clip between the two splits. Let's try it!

1. Select the video clip.
2. Position the play head just before the cursor moves to the address box. In the sample project, this occurs at about 1 minute and 17 seconds.
3. Click on the **Split** button above the timeline.
4. Select the video clip to the right of the split and move the cursor about 6 seconds later and before the CuePrompter home page appears.
5. Click on the **Split** button again.
6. Right-click on the short clip between the two splits.
7. Select **Clip speed....**

8. In the % **of original clip speed** box, type **200** and click on **OK**. The selected clip shortens to half of its original length and double the speed of movement, as shown in the following screenshot:

9. Move the trailing video left until it is snug against the adjusted clip.

10. Preview the changes and save your work.

You should see the text being typed in the box faster now, with the audio matching the action. This concludes the exercise for adjusting the clip speed.

Using visual effects

There are many visual effects available in Camtasia Studio that you can use to enhance your e-learning videos. Sporting events on TV are a good example of the effectiveness of such visual effects. Watching a major game on TV without visual effects would be a very different experience than it is, and possibly a frustrating one. Without the types of visual effects I am describing, you would need to listen carefully to know the score, the time remaining, the names of the players, and perhaps even what teams are playing. With the visual effects you will be using, the experience becomes much more informative and entertaining.

Apply these techniques to an e-learning video and you have real power to engage and inform. This section describes the use of some of the available visual effects and coaches you through exercises to reinforce your understanding. We will describe the use of four visual effects: adding transitions, inserting images, using callouts, and using the zoom and pan effects.

Adding transitions

A transition in video is a method of easing a change in scenes, inserted between visuals. For example, when using a video camera, you might record footage of one scene and then start recording a different scene right after that. When editing such footage, you could improve the viewing experience by adding a transition between the two scenes.

What are transitions?

You place a transition over the end of one video clip and the beginning of the next one to provide a smooth visual change from one to the next. Also, transitions can be placed at the beginning or end of individual clips, images, or callouts. When viewing the produced video without a transition, the scene cuts abruptly from one image to the next. While that might be appropriate for some scenes or montages where you want to switch from image to image quickly, it can be disconcerting if the context demands subtlety.

The transitions available in Camtasia Studio range from subtle to striking. A gentle **Fade** from one scene blending into the next scene is commonly used and offers a subtle but distinct visual transition. More elaborate ones, including **Spiral** and **Page turn**, convey a message of moving on from one subject to a different one.

Artists use jarring images with purpose when they have a very special, and perhaps intentionally jarring or comic, effect in mind. Using a wide variety of wild scene transitions in an e-learning video can be confusing and distracting to the viewer. The best practice is to use them sparingly.

In this exercise, we will explore the use of the **Fade** transition.

Try it – using transitions

We will insert a **Fade** transition between the title and the body of the video. In the sample project, this occurs at about 8 seconds on the timeline. Use the following steps for the **Fade** transition:

1. If the video track is locked or turned off, click on the appropriate icon on the left-hand side to unlock or turn it on.

2. Select the **Transitions** task tab.

3. Locate the **Fade** transition. Drag it over the timeline.

4. Note the yellow highlights between the title clip and the video clip. This indicates an area where you can apply a transition, as shown in the following screenshot:

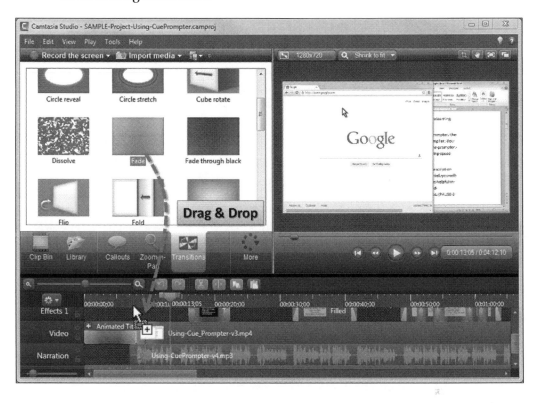

5. Drop the transition over the two clips to apply it.

6. Preview this area of the timeline to see the fade effect, where the title fades gently into the video clip.

 You can adjust the duration of the fade using the mouse. Position the cursor over one end of the fade area. When the cursor becomes a double arrow, drag the fade to change the duration, as shown in the following screenshot:

Fade transitions are good for subtle changes in a scene. To indicate a more distinct change, consider the **Fade through black** and **Page turn** transitions.

Inserting images

Camtasia Studio has a multitrack layering capability to allow producers to insert visuals on a track so they "float" over the main image on the screen. This allows you to introduce information not carried in the recorded video track. I have used this feature many times to correct a recording mistake, such as having a login pop up appear at the wrong time or in the wrong place. Just placing a screenshot of the login pop up over the video clip and positioning it on screen corrects this issue.

Try it – inserting images

In the sample video, the second sentence of the narration says, "…you will learn about CuePrompter, the free online tool that works like a TelePrompTer." This is where we will insert a downloaded image using the following steps:

 Any image, video clip, or effect placed on the timeline above the background video clip will appear in front of it since it will be on a higher layer. If placed on a lower track, it will not be visible.

1. In an Internet browser, navigate to `http://cueprompter.com/`.
2. On the CuePrompter home page, locate the thumbnail of a prompter window near the top-left corner of the page.
3. Right-click on the image and select the option to save the image. Save and store it in your project folder.
4. Locate the words that begin "...you will learn about CuePrompter" on the timeline. In the sample project, it occurs at about 16 seconds.
5. Place the play head at the start of these words.
6. Click on the **Import media** button above the **Clip Bin** panel.
7. Load the image you just downloaded to the Camtasia Studio **Clip Bin** panel.
8. Drag-and-drop the image on the timeline. It should be placed on a track above the video clip.
9. Click on a corner sizing handle and drag the image larger so the text is readable.

10. Adjust the duration to the end of the sentence. You can tell where the end is visually by the absence of wave forms on the `Narration` audio.

11. Add **Fade** transitions at the beginning and end of the imported image. It should look like the following screenshot:

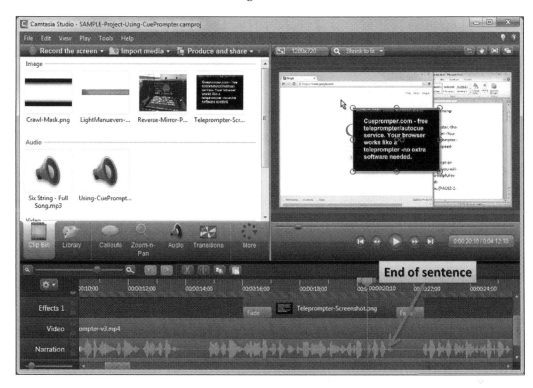

12. Preview the changes and save your work.

Layering images or even other videos above the main recording is a great way to add visual information. This exercise showed us how to do so with a screenshot. You can use the same technique with any visual asset that is compatible and can be imported into Camtasia Studio.

Always check with the owner of the assets you use. CuePrompter (`http://cueprompter.com/`) is acknowledged here and elsewhere for granting permission to use videos and images captured from their website.

Using callouts

You have a lot of options in how you "call out" information in e-learning videos. **Callouts** are typically used visually to highlight or point to something, perhaps when it is mentioned or explained in the narration. An analogy is when an instructor uses a pointer in a live presentation to draw attention to a visual detail.

The callout feature

The Camtasia Studio callout feature allows you to place and layer visual elements on the timeline and manipulate them in the preview window to enhance your video. Callouts include some very professional elements to accomplish more than just highlighting visually. Callouts available within the **Callouts** task tab include arrows, shapes, speech bubbles, pointers, textboxes, highlights, and spotlights. There are even motion shapes that appear as if drawn by hand on the screen. You can use callouts to create some very attractive visual effects.

When selected, callouts appear on the timeline at the current position of the play head and can be moved.

Try it – using callouts

This exercise includes using a textbox callout. This is a good technique to add information about what the viewer is seeing. This is similar to the technique used on TV weather programs of using a box on the screen to show the current temperature or the weather forecast.

In this Try it exercise, you will create a callout to show the lesson objectives in a textbox on the screen, as specified in the storyboard.

Selecting and designing the callout

In this part of the exercise, we will create a rounded rectangle textbox callout that uses colors compatible with the visual theme established in the title clip. Start with your exercise project open in Camtasia Studio and perform the following steps:

1. Locate the course objectives in the audio narration. In the sample project, this occurs at about 49 seconds on the timeline and says, "At the end of this video, you will be able to...."

2. Position the play head right before that sentence.

3. Select the **Callouts** task tab.

4. Click on the down arrow next to **Shape** and select the blue rounded rectangle. This places a default box on the timeline and the preview window.

5. Type your text in the box.

6. Save your project.

Customizing the callout

The second part of this Try it exercise is to customize the callout to suit your e-learning video project. The following steps are recommended as a best practice. Feel free to modify the textbox to suit your own purposes:

1. Select the callout textbox you just created.

2. Set the **Border**, **Fill**, and **Effects** controls for the callout.

 For the sample project, a white border, brown background, and a shadow were used.

3. Set the **Fade in** and **Fade out** times to **1** second.

4. Select the **Text** formatting controls to adjust text font, color, size, and other attributes.

To get bullets formatted like the ones in the following screenshot, use a word processing program such as Microsoft Word to enter and format the text, then copy and paste it from there. Your text retains the settings made in the word processing program.

5. Reposition the callout in the preview window where the box will appear on the screen in the video.

6. On the timeline, use the cursor and mouse to set when the box will first fade in on the screen and then when it will fade out.

7. Preview the changes and save your work.

Refer to the following screenshot for the location of items mentioned in this exercise:

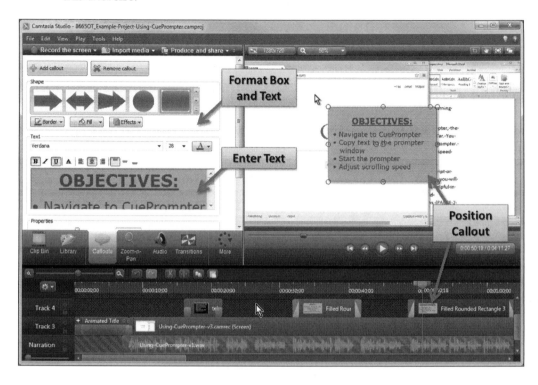

Your **Objectives** callout should look like the following screenshot:

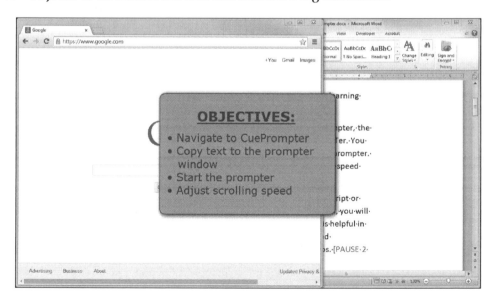

Callout extra credit

This part of the callout exercise is an optional advanced technique. So far, you have created a single callout box in this exercise with a title at the top and four bullet points that are visible the whole time the callout displays. It would be a nice bonus for the bullets to fade in as each point is mentioned in the audio file.

To see how this is done, open the `Sample-Project-Using-CuePrompter.camproj` file you have previously downloaded and unzipped.

Preview the area of the **Objectives** callout at about 48 seconds on the timeline. In this sample, the callout fades in with only the title visible at the top. Then, the four bullets fade in, one at a time, as they are mentioned in the audio. This is a good technique for keeping the viewer's interest while enumerating items. This exercise was done using the following steps:

1. In your exercise project, start with the customized callout already created.

2. Starting from the beginning of the callout, play the preview.

3. As the audio plays, create splits in the callout on the timeline at each of the following places:

   "At the end of this video, you will be able to **[SPLIT 1]** navigate to the CuePrompter website, **[SPLIT 2]** copy and paste text from your script into the prompter text window, **[SPLIT 3]** start the prompter, and **[SPLIT 4]** adjust the prompter scrolling speed."

4. Apply **Fade** transitions to each of the splits.

5. Your callout sequence should look like the following screenshot on the timeline:

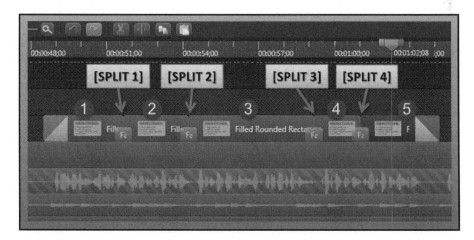

6. Now double-click on each segment of the callout sequence and edit them, as follows, by removing the parts not needed:

    1. Segment 5 should have the title and all four bullets.

    2. Segment 4 should have the title and the first three bullets.

    3. Segment 3 should have the title and the first two bullets.

    4. Segment 2 should have the title and the first bullet.

    5. Segment 1 should have only the title and no bullets.

7. Preview the changes and save your work. You will see each bullet slowly fade on screen, timed with the narration.

To help illustrate this process, refer to the sample project, which contains a segmented callout sequence like this one. If you have the previous sequence working as shown in the sample project, congratulations! You can use this technique whenever you need to animate text to appear in sequence.

That completes this Try it exercise on using callouts. You now know the basics of placing callouts on the timeline and customizing them. You also have access to an advanced technique, where text bullets are animated to appear timed with the narration.

Using zoom and pan effects

Zooming is changing the magnification of the video scene to show detail or to emphasize something. It is an excellent technique to eliminate areas of the scene that may be a distraction to viewers. Panning is moving the view across the scene without changing magnification. This could be used to show a progression from one area of the scene to another.

Here is an example of these two techniques. Imagine you are using a video camera mounted on a tripod to record a lecturer at a podium and a presentation being shown on a screen nearby. You start with a shot of the lecturer only. The lecturer begins referring to a picture in the presentation. To show the picture, you first turn the camera from the lecturer toward the screen until the image is centered in the frame. This is a panning action. Second, you use the zoom control on the camera to enlarge the screen and the image being projected. This is zooming in. And third, you use the zoom control again to enlarge the scene to show both the lecturer and the screen. This is zooming out.

The Zoom-n-Pan feature

Use the **Zoom-n-Pan** feature to zoom in, zoom out, and reposition the view of the video. This tool actually creates animations that you can control on the timeline for timing and duration, zoom level, and position on the screen.

When selected, a zoom and pan preview window opens to allow you to adjust the zoom level or position.

Camtasia Studio has the capability to simulate the previously mentioned camera techniques after the recording has been made in post production. You can learn more about this visual effect in this Try it exercise.

Try it – zooming and panning

We will apply zoom and pan to a portion of the timeline to show how to use these techniques.

Zooming in

In this part of the Try it exercise, you will apply a zoom in, which magnifies an area of the screen, using the following steps:

1. In your exercise project, move the play head to the area of the timeline just before the image that was inserted in a previous exercise.
2. Select the **Zoom-n-Pan** task tab.
3. Grab a corner resize handle and drag to make the highlight area smaller.

Referring to the upcoming screenshot, make sure you are operating in the **Zoom-n-Pan** preview, not the canvas area of the main preview window. Resizing within the canvas area is a different type of effect and may not accomplish what you want.

4. Release the resize handle when you feel the magnification is correct. The scene in the preview window shows the effect.

An effect arrow appears on the clip in the timeline, as shown in the following screenshot. Stretch this arrow to adjust the zoom duration on the timeline to a comfortable, slow zoom. The best practice is for a zoom or pan duration of at least 1 second.

5. Preview the changes without saving.

6. Keep the **Zoom-n-Pan** task tab open for now.

The changes will be displayed in the preview, as shown in the following screenshot:

Panning

In this part of the Try it exercise, you will apply a panning movement, which scrolls across an area of the screen, using the following steps:

1. In the exercise project, move the play head to another area of the timeline.

2. In the **Zoom-n-Pan** preview panel, grab and drag the highlighted zoom area toward the right.

3. Release the highlight when you feel the position is correct.

 Another effect arrow appears on the clip in the timeline.

4. Preview the changes without saving.

5. Keep the **Zoom-n-Pan** task tab open for now.

The changes will be displayed in the preview, as shown in the following screenshot:

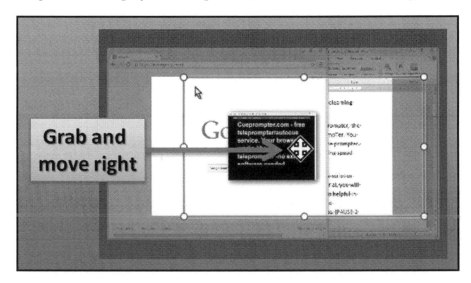

Zooming out

In this part of the Try it exercise, you will apply a zoom out, which displays a larger area of the screen, using the following steps:

1. In the sample project, move the play head to another area of the timeline.

2. In the **Zoom-n-Pan** preview panel, click on the **Scale media** button. The scene reverts to fill 100 percent of the canvas area on the preview window with the visual effect of zooming out to the original size.

 Note a third effect arrow appears on the clip in the timeline.

3. Preview the changes and save your work.

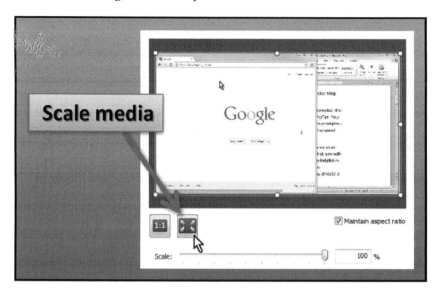

This concludes the exercise for using zoom and pan effects. Zoom and pan are visual effects that can greatly enhance your e-learning video, showing details and eliminating areas of the scene that may distract your viewers.

Summary

In this chapter, you learned how to perform edits in Camtasia Studio. Basic edits are crucial in creating a high-quality e-learning video.

We learned how to layer effects on the timeline to create rich visuals typically associated with professional **non-linear editing (NLE)** systems. These are powerful features, finally available to e-learning video authors in recent Camtasia Studio releases. They allow you to not only import video, audio, and pictures into the timeline, but you can also apply and layer visual effects, all of which do not alter your original footage, but create stunning footage in your final output.

Throughout this chapter, we saw that your original footage, pictures, and sound tracks are unaltered while editing. Editing prepares the Camtasia project file for final output, where all of the changes we have been making will be evident in execution.

Keep in mind that your original assets should be safely stored where you can find them on your computer later. Your output files will later be stored in a different place.

Now, we move on to the next chapter. It describes adding a quiz to your e-learning video project. We will focus on creating good questions, using the quiz-builder interface in Camtasia Studio, and setting your project up to report scores to a learning management system.

7
Quizzes and Interactions

This chapter covers everything required to add quizzes and other interactive features to your Camtasia Studio e-learning videos. It includes a description of how interactions are created and how they function. There are step-by-step procedures to create interactions and quizzes in Camtasia Studio. Instructions and tips to add interactivity are included. Taken together, these elements constitute the *interactive* part of learning, as practiced in an e-learning video.

In video, an interaction with learners is a request to respond to what they are seeing and hearing, mainly by selecting, clicking, or typing. These interaction instructions could be navigating to some additional or alternate information, for example, or choosing a response to a question. Up until now, in our exercises, we have created an e-learning video that is strictly a one-way communication: the information imparted in the video contents that are viewed and heard by the learner. We have no way of gauging whether this one-way flow of information has made any impact. We do not know the answer to the questions: "Has the learner gained any knowledge, information, or skill?" and "Can the learner demonstrate that they have learned something?"

As you are aware by now, interactivity and knowledge assessments are crucial in any e-learning program. Even if your plans do not include monitoring and scoring learners' responses, interactions with the e-learning program are important to keep the learner engaged in the process. Consuming a learning video without interacting is like watching a TV program. Viewers are exposed to information but they are unlikely to retain much of it long term. Research has proven interactions bolster the learning process and help students retain knowledge longer.

Many Camtasia Studio users do not realize they can incorporate interactivity into their e-learning videos. You can enhance your video as an e-learning experience using some basic features in the program to create quizzes and add interactions.

The following are some of the specific topics we will cover in this chapter:

- The types of interactions available in Camtasia Studio
- Video player requirements
- Creating simple action hotspots
- Publishing and testing your interactive output
- Using the quiz feature in Camtasia to insert a quiz or survey
- Options for scoring the quiz
- Reporting scores to a **learning management system (LMS)** or via e-mail
- Publishing and testing the interaction
- Tips and shortcuts

By the end of this chapter, you will know how to use the features available in Camtasia Studio to engage and interact with learners. You will be able to insert simple hotspot interactions and quizzes. In the latter case, you will learn how to receive quiz data from your e-learning video module. And you will know the best ways to deliver the content and test it for correct function. First, here is a brief overview of how and why interactions are effective in learning.

Why include learner interactions?

Interactions in e-learning support cognitive learning, the application of behavioral psychology to teaching. Students learn a lot when they perform an action based on the information they are presented. Without exhausting the volumes written about this subject, your own background has probably prepared you for creating effective materials that support cognitive learning. To boil it down for our purposes, you present information in chunks and ask learners to demonstrate whether they have received the signal.

In the classroom, this is immortalized as a teacher presenting a lecture and asking questions, a basic educational model. In another scenario, it might be an instructor showing a student how to perform a mechanical task and then asking the student to repeat the same task.

We know from experience that learners struggle with concepts if you present too much information too rapidly without checking to see if they understand it. In e-learning, the most effective ways to prevent confusion involve chunking information into small, digestible bites and mapping them into an overall program that allows the learner to progress in a logical fashion, all the while interacting and demonstrating comprehension.

Interaction is vital to keep your students awake and aware. Interaction, or two-way communication, can take your e-learning video to the next level: a true cognitive learning experience.

Keep this cognitive model and the basic forms of interaction in mind as we move forward in this chapter.

Interaction types

While Camtasia Studio does not pretend to be a full-featured interactive authoring tool, it does contain some features that allow you to build interactions and quizzes. This section defines those features that support learners to take action while viewing an e-learning video when you request them for an interaction.

There are three types of interactions available in Camtasia Studio:

- Simple action hotspots
- Branching hotspots
- Quizzes

You are probably thinking of ways these techniques can help support cognitive learning.

This book does not cover mapping and creating branching schemes. An example is a branch menu, a simple fork with three options. The learner clicks on one, reviews the content, and either clicks back to the branch menu or goes to the next alternate branch. For a tutorial and instructions for creating a branched e-learning module in Camtasia Studio, go to http://www.spectorial.com/branching.html.

Simple action hotspots

Hotspots are click areas. You indicate where the hotspot is using a visual cue, such as a callout. Camtasia allows you to designate the area covered by the callout as a hotspot and define the action to take when it is clicked. An example is to take the learner to another time in the video when the hotspot is clicked. Another click could take the learner back to the original place in the video.

Quizzes

Quizzes are simple questions you can insert in the video, created and implemented to conform to your testing strategy, as explained later in this chapter. The question types available are as follows:

- Multiple choice
- Fill in the blanks
- Short answers
- True/false

Video player requirements

Before we learn how to create interactions in Camtasia Studio, you should know some special video player requirements. A simple video file playing on a computer cannot be interactive by itself. A video created and produced in Camtasia Studio without including some additional program elements cannot react when you click on it except for what the video player tells it to do. For example, the default player for YouTube videos stops and starts the video when you click anywhere in the video space.

Click interactions in videos created with Camtasia are able to recognize where clicks occur and the actions to take. You provide the click instructions when you set up the interaction. These instructions are required, for example, to intercept the clicking action, determine where exactly the click occurred, and link that spot with a command and destination. These click instructions may be any combination of **HyperText Markup Language (HTML)**, HTML5, JavaScript, and Flash ActionScript. Camtasia takes care of creating the coding behind the scenes, associated with the video player being used. In the case of videos produced with Camtasia Studio, to implement any form of interactivity, you need to select the default **Smart Player** output options when producing the video.

 There is a good overview of the TechSmith Smart Player available in Camtasia Studio **Help**. Search for the topic About TechSmith Smart Player to gain a better understanding. In the help topic, there are also links to other information at http://www.techsmith.com.

I will go over the options available for using the Smart Player options a little later.

 You will not be able to view your interactions in **Local Playback**. You must upload the video and player to a website or an LMS that is able to interpret the scripting commands being used, even when you are using the TechSmith Smart Player. There will be more information about this later.

Creating simple hotspots

The most basic interaction is clicking a hotspot layered over the video. You can create an interactive hotspot for many purposes, including the following:

- Taking learners to a specific marker or frame within the video, as determined on the timeline
- Allowing learners to replay a section of the video
- Directing learners to a website or document to view reference material
- Showing a pop up with additional information, such as a phone number or web link

Try it – creating a hotspot

If you are building the exercise project featured in this book, let's use it to create an interactive hotspot. The task in this exercise is to pause the video and add a **Replay** button to allow viewers to review a task. After the replay, a prompt will be added to resume the video from where it was paused.

Inserting the Replay/Continue buttons

The first step is to insert a **Replay** button to allow viewers to review what they just saw or continue without reviewing. This involves adding two hotspot buttons on the timeline, which can be done by performing the following steps:

1. Open your exercise project in Camtasia Studio or one of your own projects where you can practice.

> If you are following along with exercises in the sample project, a good place to insert a replay sequence is right after the copy-and-paste activity, where the script text is copied from Word and pasted into CuePrompter.

2. Position the play head right after the part where text is shown being pasted into the CuePrompter window.

> Make sure the play head is positioned in an area where the narration is silent, between sentences. In the sample audio file, you will hear the words "Next, press *Ctr l+ V* to paste your script text." Position the play head on the timeline right after you hear these words.

3. From the **Properties** area, select **Callouts** from the task tabs above the timeline.

4. In the **Shape** area, select **Filled Rounded Rectangle** (at the upper-right corner of the drop-down selection). A shape is added to the timeline.

5. Set the **Fade in** and **Fade out** durations to about half a second.

6. Select the **Effects** dropdown and choose **Style**.

7. Choose the **3D Edge** style. It looks like a raised button.

8. Set any other formatting so the button looks the way you want in the preview window.

9. In the **Text** area, type your button text. For the sample project, enter `Replay Copy & Paste`.

10. Select the button in the preview window and make a copy of the button. You can use *Ctrl + C* to copy and *Ctrl + V* to paste the button.

11. In the second copy of the button, select the text and retype it as `Continue`. It should be stacked on the timeline as shown in the following screenshot:

12. Select the **Continue** button in the preview window and drag it to the right-hand side, at the same height and distance from the edge. The final placement of the buttons is shown in the sample project.

13. Save the project.

Adding a hotspot to the Continue button

The buttons are currently inactive images on the timeline. Viewers could click them in the produced video, but nothing would happen. To make them active, enable the **Hotspot** properties for each button. To add a hotspot to the **Continue** button, perform the following steps:

1. With the **Continue** button selected, select the **Make hotspot** checkbox in the **Callouts** panel.

2. Click on the **Hotspot Properties...** button to set properties for the callout button.

3. Under **Actions**, make sure to select **Click to continue**.

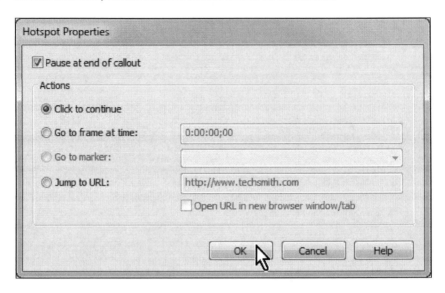

4. Click on **OK**.

The **Continue** button now has an active hotspot assigned to it. When published, the video will pause when the button appears. When the viewer clicks on **Continue**, the video will resume playing.

Adding a hotspot to the Replay button

Now, let's move on to create an action for the **Replay copy & paste** button:

1. Select the **Replay copy & paste** button in the preview window.

2. Select the **Make hotspot** checkbox in the **Callouts** panel.

3. Click on the **Hotspot properties...** button.

4. Under **Actions**, select **Go to frame at time**.

5. Enter the time code for the spot on the timeline where you want to start the replay. In the sample video, this is around 0:01:43;00, just before text is copied in the script.

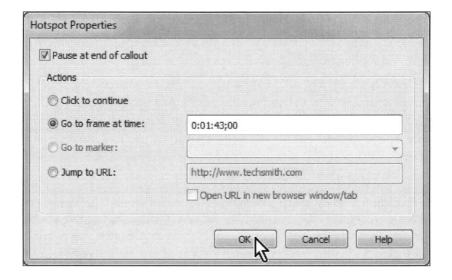

6. Click on **OK**.

7. Save the project.

The **Replay copy & paste** button now has an active hotspot assigned to it. Later, when published, the video will pause when the button appears. When viewers click on **Replay copy & paste**, the video will be repositioned at the time you entered and begin playing from there. You can test the video and the operation of the interactive buttons as described later in this chapter.

Using the quiz feature

A quiz added to a video sets it apart. The addition of knowledge checks and quizzes to assess your learners' understanding of the material presented puts the video into the true e-learning category.

By definition, a **knowledge check** is a way for the student to check their understanding without worrying about scoring. Typically, feedback is given to the student for them to better understand the material, the question, and their answer. The feedback can be terse, such as correct and incorrect, or it can be verbose, informing if the answer is correct or not and perhaps giving additional information, a hint, or even the correct answers, depending on your strategy in creating the knowledge check.

A **quiz** can be in the same form as a knowledge check but a record of the student's answer is created and reported to an LMS or via an e-mail report. Feedback to the student is optional, again depending on your testing strategy.

In Camtasia Studio, you can insert a quiz question or set of questions anywhere on the timeline you deem appropriate. This is done with the **Quizzing** task tab.

Try it – inserting a quiz

In this exercise, you will select a spot on the timeline to insert a quiz, enable the **Quizzing** feature, and write some appropriate questions following the sample project, *Using CuePrompter*.

Creating a quiz

Place your quiz after you have covered a block of information. The sample project, *Using CuePrompter*, is a very short task-based tutorial, showing some basic steps. Assume for now that you are teaching a course on CuePrompter and need to assess students' knowledge. I believe a good place for a quiz is after the commands to scroll forward, speed up, slow down, and scroll reverse. Let's give it a try with multiple choice and true/false questions:

1. Position the play head at the appropriate part of the timeline. In the sample video, the end of the scrolling command description is at about 3 minutes 12 seconds.

2. Select **Quizzing** in the task tabs. If you do not see the **Quizzing** tab above the timeline, select the **More** tab to reveal it.

3. Click on the **Add quiz** button to begin adding questions. A marker appears on the timeline where your quiz will appear during the video, as illustrated in the following screenshot:

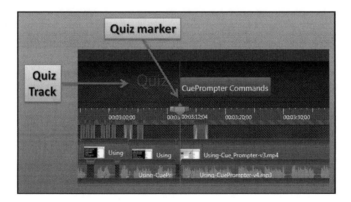

4. In the **Quiz** panel, add a quiz name. In the sample project, the quiz is entitled CuePrompter Commands.

5. Scroll down to **Question type**. Make sure **Multiple Choice** is selected from the dropdown.

6. In the **Question** box, type the question text. In the sample project, the first question is `With text in the prompter ready to go, the keyboard control to start scrolling forward is _____`.

7. In the **Answers** box, double-click on the checkbox text that says **Default Answer Text**. Retype the answer `Control-F`.

8. In the next checkbox text that says **<Type an answer choice here>**, double-click on it and add the second possible answer, `Spacebar`. Check the box next to it to indicate that it is the correct answer.

9. Add two more choices: `Alt-Insert` and `Tab`.

10. Your **Quiz** panel should look like the following screenshot:

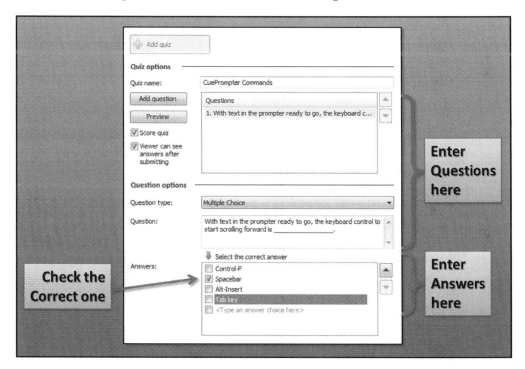

11. Click on **Add question**.

12. From the **Question type** dropdown, select **True/False**.

13. In the **Question** box, type `You can stop CuePrompter with the End key`.

14. In **Answers**, select `False`.

15. For the final question, click on **Add question** again.

16. From the **Question type** dropdown, select **Multiple Choice**.

17. In the **Question** box, type `Which keyboard command tells CuePrompter to reverse?`.

18. Enter the four possible answers:

    ○   `Left arrow`

    ○   `Right arrow`

    ○   `Down arrow`

    ○   `Up arrow`

19. Select **Down arrow** as the correct answer.

20. Save the project.

Now you have entered three questions and answer choices, while indicating the choice that will be scored correct if selected. Next, preview the quiz to check format and function.

Previewing the quiz

Camtasia Studio allows you to preview quizzes for correct formatting, wording, and scoring. Continue to follow along in the exercise project and perform the following steps:

1. Leave checkmarks in the **Score quiz** and **Viewer can see answers after submitting** boxes.

2. Click on the **Preview** button. A web page opens in your Internet browser showing the questions, as shown in the following screenshot:

3. Select an answer and click on **Next**. The second quiz question is displayed.

4. Select an answer and click on **Next**. The third quiz question is displayed.

5. Select an answer and click on **Submit Answers**. As this is the final question, there is no **Next**.

6. Since we left the **Score quiz** and **Viewer can see answers after submitting** options selected, the learner receives a prompt, as shown in the following screenshot:

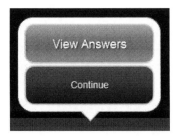

7. Click on **View Answers** to review the answers you gave. Correct responses are shown with a green checkmark and incorrect ones are shown with a red X mark.

 If you do not want your learners to see the answers, remove the checkmark from **Viewer can see answers after submitting**.

8. Exit the browser to discontinue previewing the quiz.

9. Save the project.

This completes the Try it exercise for inserting and previewing a quiz in your video e-learning project. Next, we will cover scoring the quizzes in your video.

Scoring options

If you decide scoring is required, Camtasia is capable of communicating the responses back to you, either through an **LMS** or by automatically sending an e-mail containing the quiz taker's responses.

Using SCORM

Publishing your e-learning video to an LMS to record scores requires selecting the Smart Player and SCORM options when producing the final video. This section describes how to set up your video for an LMS using the exercise sample.

Try it – setting SCORM options

This exercise will go through the publication process showing the correct options to select to report quiz scores using SCORM. This process produces a zipped file that can be uploaded to any SCORM-compliant LMS. For the exercise, we will load and test our output on **SCORM Cloud**, a free testing service that operates as a temporary LMS.

Producing the SCORM output

Use this Try it exercise to experiment with producing the SCORM output. There is a good tutorial on this feature at `http://www.techsmith.com/tutorial-camtasia-8-scorm-packages.html`. Use the following steps to produce your SCORM output:

1. With the exercise sample video open in Camtasia Studio, click on the **Produce and share** button near the top.

2. On the **Production Wizard** welcome screen, select **MP4 with Smart Player** from the dropdown.

3. Click on **Next**.

4. On the **Quiz Reporting Options** screen, select **Report quiz results using SCORM**.

5. Uncheck **Report quiz results through email**.

[

If you want to try out your quiz with a few students, you can test it using the **Report quiz results through email** option. This option is described later in this chapter.
]

6. Click on **SCORM options...**. The **Manifest Options** dialog opens.

7. Set manifest options similar to the ones shown in the following screenshot:

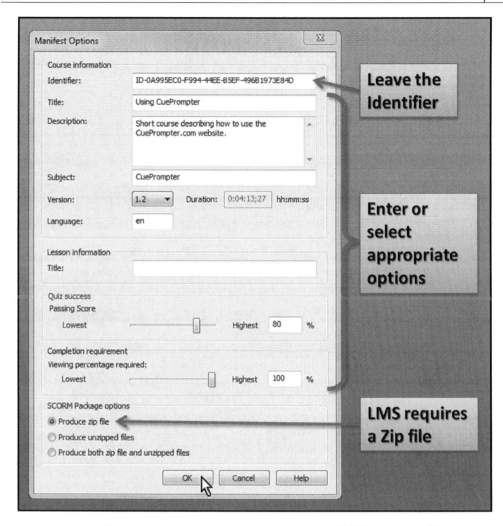

8. Click on **OK**.

9. Then, click on **Next**.

10. On the **Produce Video** screen, enter the filename and production folder.

11. Click on **Finish**.

12. Your video begins rendering and the SCORM package is prepared.

13. Save the project.

14. Note the location of the ZIP file that was created. You will need this for the next portion, testing your SCORM-compliant video and quiz.

Testing the SCORM package

If you have access to an LMS, you can test the SCORM package that you created in the *Producing the SCORM output* section. However, if you do not yet have an LMS, you can test the SCORM package at a free SCORM testing website. The following steps show how to test the SCORM package:

1. Go to `https://cloud.scorm.com`.

2. If you are not registered here, set up a free account.

 Using SCORM Cloud is not within the scope of this book. Click on the **Help** link in the upper-right corner of the SCORM Cloud page to learn how to upload and test the SCORM content.

3. When you click on **Add Content**, choose the SCORM package ZIP file you created in the *Producing the SCORM output* section of this exercise.

4. After uploading, launch the course within SCORM Cloud.

5. View the video and take the quiz. You should see the results, which will look like the following screenshot:

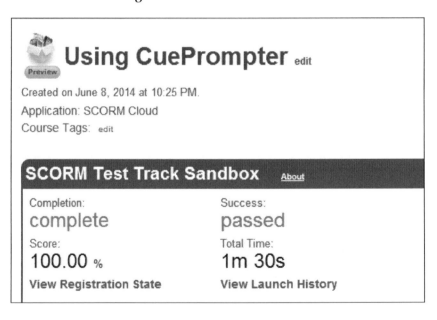

Congratulations! You have created a SCORM-compliant course. Refer to your LMS documentation for instructions to test, upload content, and register students for your own courses.

Using the e-mail scoring option

TechSmith built some capabilities into Camtasia Studio and their own servers to give you a unique and powerful option for course score management. With no investment in an LMS, you can have learners' scores e-mailed to any address you wish, with some helpful data management options available now.

 Using e-mail scoring will send a message containing the results to the e-mail account you specify. This is a good way to become familiar with the type of data being reported.

To learn more about receiving e-mail reports of learners' scores, see the tutorial at `http://www.techsmith.com/tutorial-camtasia-8-quiz-results.html`.

Publishing and testing

Interactive videos created in Camtasia Studio will work correctly when they are published using the correct options. You have three options to publish interactive videos. You can produce your video as follows:

1. To an output option that includes the TechSmith Smart Player and then publish the output to a website that can take advantage of the interactive features.

2. For publication to an LMS using the Smart Player, SCORM option, and zipped output.

3. Using the **Share to Screencast.com** production option.

One way to make sure that your interactive video tests and publishes correctly is to upload it to the TechSmith Screencast.com streaming site. Once you have established a free account there, this is easy to do from the Camtasia **Production Wizard**.

Publishing non-quiz interactions

Non-quiz interactions include those with closed captions, table of contents, or clickable hotspots. These interactions will function on a self-maintained website that is capable of interpreting the interactions when published to an LMS or when uploaded to TechSmith Screencast.com (`http://www.screencast.com/`).

For more information on how interactions work in playback, refer to the Camtasia **Help** topic **About TechSmith Smart Player**. There are links to other important topics at http://www.techsmith. com.

For this exercise, we will explore publishing your interactive video to TechSmith Screencast.com. If you do not already have a free account at TechSmith Screencast. com, you will be prompted to create one.

Try it – publishing to TechSmith Screencast. com

Use the following steps to test your produced videos for interactivity and to publish them in final form for others to view:

1. With your exercise project open in Camtasia Studio, click on the **Produce and share** button near the top.

2. On the **Production Wizard**, select **Share to Screencast.com** from the dropdown.

3. Click on **Next**. The **Sign In** screen opens.

4. Enter your Screencast login credentials.

There is a handy link to sign up for a free Screencast account on the **Sign In** screen.

5. Click on **Next**. The **Upload** screen opens.

6. From the **Screencast.com folder** dropdown, select the target folder. If it is not already available on Screencast, select **New Folder** and create one.

7. Click on **Options**. Review and set the following options:

    °   **Controller**: This option sets how the controller should behave. For our interactive test, the default selections are fine.

    °   **Size**: This is the video size. Leave the default **1280x720** video output size.

- **Video settings**: These are the video settings (video output quality). For testing, the options shown here should work fine. Your files will upload quicker and stream in playback more reliably at these quality settings. Use higher settings for better quality playback, keeping in mind the cost will be larger file sizes. You will see all the options in the following screenshot:

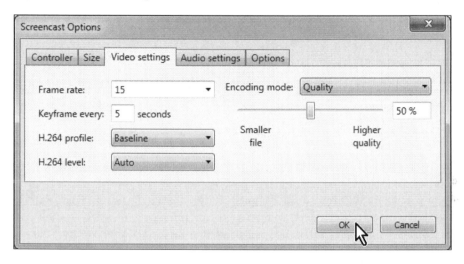

- **Audio settings**: These are the audio settings (audio output quality). The default settings are fine.

- **Options**: This is for additional features you may have included. The default settings are fine.

8. Click on **OK** to close the **Screencast Options** window.

9. Click on **Finish**. Status dialog boxes open to show production and upload progress.

10. The **Production Results** window opens. Note that there are two lines of code on this page.

11. To preserve the location of the video, click on the **Video URL** code to copy the code.

12. To embed the video player on another web page, for example, on your personal website, click on the **Embed** code to copy the code.

The embed code creates an iFrame, a web page building block, to house the Smart Player and video. After copying this code, paste it on your web page. To see an example of the embedded video code working on my consulting website, go to `http://www.spectorial.com/trainingsamples.html`.

13. Save the project.

This concludes the Try it exercise for publishing your e-learning video to TechSmith Screencast.com, a good option for streaming your video, either directly from Screencast or embedding it within another web page.

Summary

This chapter prepared you for creating interactivity, adding a quiz, and publishing your e-learning video effectively to take advantage of these features. Video without interactive elements may be fine for teaching some subjects, but you can better ensure your learners will retain the content if they are invited to interact with it, reviewing information if needed, answering quiz questions, or even branching to alternate topics. Camtasia Studio has features enabling all of these activities.

The best way to learn how to use the interactive features professionally and effectively is to practice. If you need to reinforce your knowledge and skills, revisit this chapter and practice the exercises until you feel comfortable using the interactive features.

For some situations, Camtasia Studio may be the only tool you will need to create professional interactive content including lessons and assessments. Adding your Camtasia-produced content to an LMS activates the quizzing feature and allows you to sign up students and keep track of their progress.

The next chapter will describe even more options for deploying your e-learning video to a website or an LMS.

8

Deploying Your E-learning Video to the Web or LMS

So far, you have learned about creating your e-learning video using Camtasia Studio. The forgoing topics are good to know and certainly take you most of the way. However, without deployment, your e-learning video will never be used.

This chapter will go over the steps required to produce the final output for delivery to consumers using a standard website, video streaming site, or a **learning management system (LMS)**. There are production steps to be taken within Camtasia Studio to prepare for any kind of deployment. Depending on the selections you make during the production steps, your video may be targeted to a specific streaming service, prepared for a website, or may be enabled to communicate with a learning service for scoring and completion management.

The decisions you make when deploying your content can make a huge difference in how often it is viewed and the quality viewers see. Sending a low-quality video to a premium streaming service does not take advantage of the knowledge and effort you have put into it. Deploying an e-learning video without enabling interactivity reduces it to a viewing experience that might not accomplish your viewers' learning objectives. So, you will need to make informed decisions in the production and deployment stages.

By the end of this chapter, you will know more about preparing your video production for deployment. For noninteractive videos, production steps to create your video for a streaming service or standard website will be described. For e-learning videos with interactivity, the concepts of capturing learners' interactions will be explained. What you need to know about creating SCORM-compliant output will also be described.

This chapter covers the following topics:

- Capturing learners' actions
- Hosting courses in an LMS and the LMS standards supporting that hosting environment
- Using a Moodle-based LMS
- What enterprise LMS is and how it compares with other LMS options
- Setting Camtasia Studio production options
- Testing the project
- Tips and shortcuts

Capturing the actions of learners

As you have noted in previous chapters, capturing actions from viewers sets your e-learning video apart as a true interactive learning experience. So far, we have discussed the features that enable interactivity. Interactivity means we can allow the learners to take an action, such as clicking on the video as it is playing, and the video player will react by performing certain commands. In our samples, we built a simple interaction to replay a short section of video so that viewers can review the information.

Why track learner actions?

So we know allowing video interaction is good. What about keeping track of those actions? The question inevitably follows, "If the learner can interact with the video, how can we keep track of what he or she did?" And of course, if you allow them to take a quiz within the video, it would be good to know if they answered the questions correctly or incorrectly.

Tracking can allow you to direct the learner in ways that you cannot with a standard streaming service such as YouTube or Vimeo. For example, you can set up a special branching order of modules where completion of one enables the next required course.

These tracking, scoring, and certifying tasks require the exchange of data. You need to capture and keep track of those learner decisions, clicks, and answers. We'll see in a moment how this tracking is enabled.

What is certification?

A higher level of tracking the results of learner interactions is the special case of certification. At the end of the learning experience, if your learners need to provide a record they succeeded in completion at the minimum acceptable grade level or higher, they are said to be certified. A diploma from a university is a form of certification. The institution is willing to state on record that the learner has demonstrated mastery of the subjects studied.

Certification requirements are common for compliance training, such as safety or wage-and-hour training, and manual job skills training, such as driving a forklift. The certification provides a strong incentive to the education department to keep track of how well the learner demonstrated their mastery of the subjects.

How is interaction of data used?

As we covered in *Chapter 7, Quizzes and Interactions*, a simple streaming video is not equipped to transmit the data required to keep track of the interactions. Our authoring tools, Camtasia Studio included, can produce the data in the form of SCORM-compliant output. Up until now, we have not discussed the receiving end of this data. This is where an LMS becomes important. If you have a need to know how well or poorly a learner did in the e-learning experience, you may need an LMS.

There are plenty of LMS packages available in the market, with various capabilities and price ranges. There are even some good free ones.

 To learn more about open source and low-cost LMS options, perform a web search using `Free LMS` as the search term. Also, refer to `http://moodle.org`.

This raises another possibility. If you do not want the expense or extra work involved in operating an LMS, and if the total number of learners is relatively low, you could consider the e-mail reporting option described in *Chapter 7, Quizzes and Interactions*. This reporting is adequate for many situations.

If you are setting up an online course, look at the various options to administer your efforts before creating a lot of content. The decision-making algorithm here, then, could be stated as follows:

> "*Given the class size and budget, plus my time availability for the manual duties required without an LMS, balanced against the extra duties required to administer an LMS, should I invest in one?*"

The only way to know is to be informed and try out various options. Consider starting with the free options, using an open source LMS or trying to manage the Camtasia e-mail score reporting option. If those solutions become unmanageable, then look to invest in a cloud-based LMS with a tiered pricing structure. But be aware that automation comes with the necessity of administering it.

Hosting courses in an LMS

For those who routinely work with an LMS, know that Camtasia Studio supports the uploading of your video content to the LMS as a lesson module. This means Camtasia packages your video for online distribution through a method called **SCORM**, which stands for **Shareable Content Object Reference Model**.

SCORM interface standard

SCORM is a standard for deploying e-learning content over a network (either the Web or a corporate intranet). It allows your web-based lessons to communicate with your LMS, regardless of which one you use. SCORM is the standard used to deploy these learning modules and can be set up to track learner progress. There is more information in *Chapter 7, Quizzes and Interactions*, about setting the scoring options in e-learning videos produced using Camtasia Studio.

How does SCORM work?

When your video is produced from Camtasia Studio with SCORM data, a special zipped package is created for uploading to a SCORM-compliant learning system. This package contains everything needed to set the course up for proper communication within the LMS. A manifest file is included that contains all of the information the LMS needs to gather data from the learners' actions within the course. There are other assorted files in the SCORM package the LMS uses to activate the interactive features and obtain the data needed. Any interactions learners perform with the content are recorded and passed back to the LMS for record-keeping and reporting.

SCORM is the language that makes all of this possible. It sets the standard for communication between interactive courses and learning management systems. Most LMS vendors certify their systems to be SCORM compliant, which means that if you create SCORM-compliant output, it should work well with their system.

If you are ever in doubt about a particular system's ability to host your content successfully, with all features working as promised, make sure to request a test. Produce your files and follow the vendor's instructions to test them within their system. This will prevent a lot of headaches down the road.

The AICC and Tin Can interfaces

Camtasia Studio does not directly support AICC or Tin Can interfaces. However, their descriptions are included to give you a more complete picture.

AICC stands for **Aviation Industry CBT Committee** and, in reference to AICC-coded learning content, means it will work in a system that supports these standards. AICC is a bit more than an LMS standard. It provides a method of intersystem communication so that learning content from one system will work in another compliant system. This enables playing AICC-compliant learning content within another system as if it were sourced on one system. This technique allows content providers to stream their modules in multiple systems, for example, selling the content to several clients who purchase it to play on their own systems.

Tin Can, also known as the **Experience API**, is a fairly new method that basically enriches the SCORM standards. It was renamed Experience API because it collects many more data points about learners' experiences while interacting with content from older standards. Rather than working with a limited dataset, Tin Can sends statements about all learner interactions to a **Learning Record Store** (**LRS**). This provides almost limitless recording of any data the content creator would like to know about. If you are seeking rich analytical data about your learners and their interactions with your content, consider researching this interface, supported by an increasing number of content authoring tools and learning management systems.

At the date this book is written, Camtasia Studio does not directly interface with the Experience API. But Camtasia-produced videos can stream in many learning management systems that also have their own quizzing interface and do utilize the Experience API. And my own tip: make sure the selected LMS vendor also offers an analytics engine that can take advantage of all the experience data you decide to collect.

For more information on AICC, refer to http://www.aicc.org/. For information on Tin Can, refer to http://tincanapi.com/overview/.

Using a Moodle-based LMS

One of the most popular ways for organizations to host their learning content is to use a Moodle-based system. Moodle is an open and free software system designed to host interactive learning content such as the ones produced by Camtasia Studio and other authoring software. Briefly, the advantage of using a Moodle-based LMS is that Moodle is available as a free download. The disadvantage is that Moodle is more of a do-it-yourself approach—unless you pay someone to customize it for you, it may not be as flexible as you would like. Many education systems use Moodle and already have it set up for easy course upload and administration. If you are an educator, you may not need to worry about the issues of setting up and administering the learning system.

If you are the person responsible for Moodle set up and administration, you must know some things about how to download, install, operate, and administer such a system if you use the free option. Paid options such as edX, Moodlerooms, and Blackboard are available that may provide you a solution that costs less than the enterprise systems described in the upcoming section.

 As Moodle supports SCORM-compliant content, your Camtasia interactive videos should work fine. As mentioned previously, testing is the only way to ensure your content will operate with your chosen Moodle system.

Enterprise systems

There are many learning systems aimed at the commercial market. These systems, available in many service models, offer clients a stable, flexible way to host content. This may be appropriate for organizations that are not interested in building and customizing their own system and are looking for a vendor to build and maintain their LMS. The trend today is toward systems that do not reside on client premises, but rather are hosted on the **cloud**. Vendors provide a way for clients to host content in a secure **multitenant** environment. This means the software is set up to virtually provide the same features to many clients while keeping each one's content and data separate and secure. Your learners log on as they would when using a company-owned system, unaware that they are using a rented space.

There are many advantages to using an enterprise system for organizations that can afford it. Basically, the vendor is responsible for building and maintaining the system, upgrading on a regular basis to include features demanded by all of their paying clients. The competitive market for such systems is fierce, so features tend to be added rapidly in a quest to gain and hold clients.

The only real disadvantage to an enterprise LMS is cost. They tend to cost more than a do-it-yourself approach. However, small organizations can find feature-rich learning management services at a very reasonable monthly cost and in a small-scale solution.

Setting production options

For this section, we switch back to Camtasia Studio and present a description of how to set production options when producing your final video. When your e-learning video is done and you are happy with how it looks when previewed on the Camtasia timeline, you can produce the final output.

In *Chapter 6, Editing the Project*, there was an explanation of how files that are imported into Camtasia Studio are not modified in the editing process. The Camtasia project file maintains links to those files and creates a separate copy of the video footage.

The same is true in the reverse scenario during production. In the production step, Camtasia produces another file or set of files that are completely new. They are in no way linked with the original assets, except with those nondestructive links in the Camtasia project file. In the simplest model, Camtasia creates a new, separate movie file that represents all of the edits and effects you created on the timeline.

This section describes the settings you make when producing your final output. The settings are different for creating a single movie file and for using the TechSmith Smart Player, so two Try it exercises are included here.

 To produce an interactive e-learning video with Camtasia Studio, your only option is to select the Smart Player production options. Preparing your project for this type of output is described in *Chapter 7, Quizzes and Interactions*.

Try it – producing a single movie file

A single video file without interactivity may be used if your goal is to upload your video to a streaming service or to play your video locally on your computer. Camtasia is able to produce a variety of output formats including Windows Media (WMV), Apple QuickTime (MOV), and Audio/Video Interleave (AVI). However, most streaming services today accept MP4 videos and most computer-based players will play them just fine. Many video producers like to avoid the platform-specific file types such as Windows Media or QuickTime simply because using them may force viewers to download another movie player they have no need for, except to view their video. For simplicity, this Try it exercise shows how to set the options to create a single MP4 movie file. You have the flexibility to produce your MP4 movie file at any size. You can also use the presets for **480p** and **720p**. Selecting one of these will ensure that your video plays at maximum quality for the streaming service or web player you use:

 If you have followed along in the previous chapters, you have a completed video project file ready for final production. If you do not have access to that file, try the upcoming exercise steps with the provided sample project.

1. Start with a completed open project file.
2. Click on the **Produce and share** button above the clip bin. The **Production Wizard** opens.

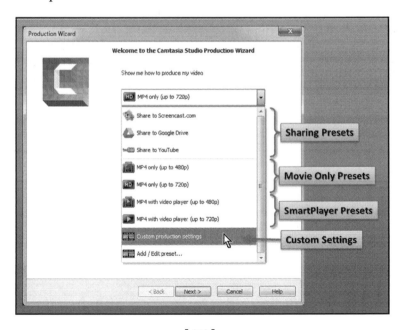

3. For this exercise, click on the production preset dropdown and select **Custom production settings**.

You can also get good results using the other MP4 production presets. I am using the custom selection so that you can review the many options available.

4. Click on **Next**. The format selection wizard panel opens.

5. The **Recommended** option is **MP4 – Flash / HTML5 player**.

TechSmith recommends this production format because they know it is widely accepted and generally trouble-free. Choose one of the other options if your situation demands it.

6. Click on **Next**.

7. On the **Flash / HTML5 Player Options** page, a tabbed dialog appears with many selections available. We will go through the most important ones.

Don't let the name of the window fool you. You can turn off the Smart Player options and produce a single movie file.

8. On the **Controller** tab, uncheck **Produce with controller**. We will explore that option in the next Try it exercise.

9. Select the **Size** tab. Review the **Width** and **Height** fields under **Video size** to make sure your final movie will be produced with the correct dimensions. Make sure there is a checkmark in the **Keep aspect ratio** box.

If you follow the advice elsewhere in this book, you will want to produce your final movie with the same dimensions and aspect ratio as your recordings and editing settings. This creates the best quality output without scaling.

10. Select the **Video settings** tab.

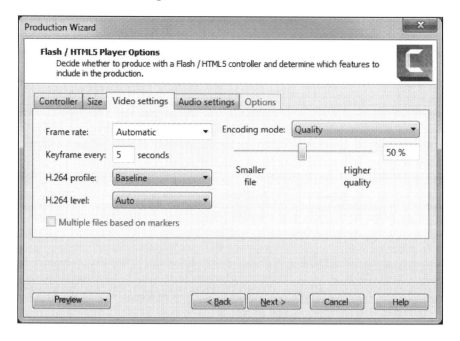

11. The following are the most important options on the **Video settings** tab.

   ○ **Frame rate**: The **Automatic** option is always safe because it produces a video using the highest frame rate of all clips on the timeline. Set a lower rate if file size is an issue. The lower the frame rate, the smaller the file will be. Dropping frame rate may cause a jerky appearance, especially when showing rapid movements.

   ○ **Encoding mode**: This should be left at the **Quality** setting. Set the slider to at least 50%. The smaller quality percentages produce smaller video files and reduced visual quality.

To preserve the highest quality in videos to be uploaded to a streaming site such as YouTube, Vimeo, or TechSmith Screencast.com, set the **Quality** setting at **100%**. This may produce a very large file and it may take a while to upload, but it gives the streaming service the best quality to start with, which is then compressed by their software. You will be very pleased with how these videos look.

Resist the urge to use the **Bitrate** setting and force your video output to a low setting for the sake of a quick download. Many good, clear videos are ruined in this quest, turning them into an unrecognizable blur. Smaller bitrates create smaller video files with much lower visual quality.

○ The default **Keyframe every** setting of **5** is fine and should not be changed unless you are desperate to reduce the file size. A higher number here will reduce the size of your files by a small percentage.

○ Leave the default settings for **H.264 profile** and **H.264 level**.

12. Select the **Audio settings** tab. Make sure that **Encode audio** is checked.

> The audio **Bitrate** setting determines the sound quality. Setting the bit rate too low produces a smaller file. I recommend a **Bitrate** setting of no lower than 96 kbps. If you are using music, consider an even higher setting.

13. Click on **Next**.

14. On the **Produce Video** page, type an output name and select a folder to store it. Set the remainder of the options to suit your purposes.

15. Click on **Finish**. The **Rendering Project** pop up shows how long the process should take. Generally, the longer the video, the longer the rendering process will take.

16. You will be informed when rendering is complete. The video preview will begin playing.

17. Click on **Finish** again.

18. Don't forget to save your project one last time.

Review the video to make sure it represents exactly what you expected. If not, you can make more changes in Camtasia Studio and go through the production steps again until it is perfect. This concludes the Try it exercise for producing a single video using the **Flash / HTML 5 Player Options** page, but without the player.

Try it – producing video with Smart Player

There are two main reasons to select the Smart Player production options, as follows:

- The first reason is to create a package that includes the player and a web page to house the video. This is handy for users who want to post the video on a private website.

- The second reason is to produce a video with interactive features such as quizzes, hotspots, or a table of contents. Note that Smart Player is required for interactive e-learning videos.

When selecting this option, Camtasia creates an MP4 video that is identical to the one produced as a standalone video file. Enabling the Smart Player option also automatically creates a video player and assorted other files such as Flash and JavaScript to enable the interactive features. Let's start performing the following steps:

1. Start with a completed project file opened in Camtasia Studio.

2. The steps for working with **Production Wizard** are the same as shown in the *Try it – producing a single movie file* section until you reach the **MP4 – Flash / HTML5 Player Options** page.

3. On the **Controller** tab, ensure that **Produce with controller** is checked. This option creates the Smart Player for your video.

4. Select the **Controller theme** dropdown. For this exercise, select the **Matte** option.

 You can preview the various player controls by selecting them from the **Controller theme** dropdown.

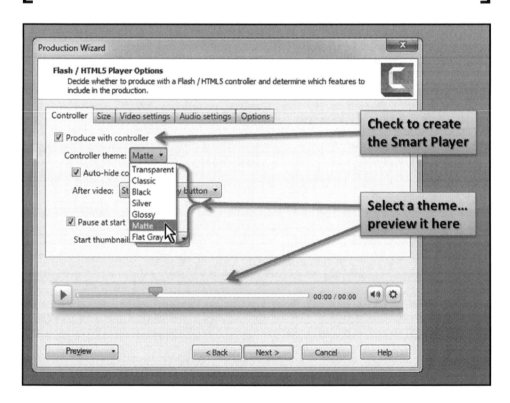

5. Most of the default settings for other options on this page are fine.

6. If you wish to change the thumbnail image used when the video is paused at the beginning, you can do so here. Click on the **Start thumbnail** dropdown and select an image to use as a thumbnail.

7. To review settings made on the other tabs, go to the *Try it – producing a single movie file* section.

8. Click on the **Options** tab to review the settings. The following are the most important options in the **Options** tab:

   ° **Table of contents**: Select this option if you have included markers on the timeline that you want to use as entries in the table of contents, to be displayed to the left of the video.

   ° **Searchable**: This creates a search pane to the left of the video and allows the viewer to search for text within captions.

   ° **Captions**: Select this option if you have enabled and entered text for captioning. You can select the **Caption type** option (**Closed** captions, **Burned in** captions, or **Under video** captions) and check **Captions initially visible** if you want them to appear by default. If selected, viewers will need to turn them off if they are unwanted.

   ° **Quizzing**: Check this option to enable quizzing if you have included one in the project.

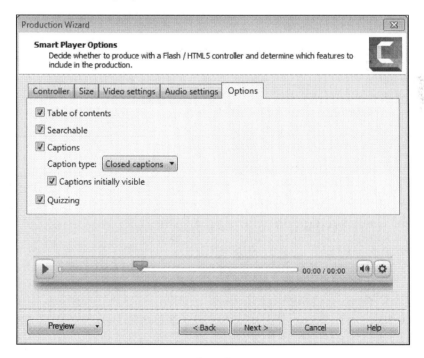

9. Click on **Next**.

 If you are producing an e-learning video for an LMS, refer to *Chapter 7, Quizzes and Interactions*, for instructions on those settings.

10. Click on **Next**. Type an output name and select a folder to store it.

11. Click on **Finish**. The **Rendering Project** pop up shows how long the process should take. Generally, the longer the video and the more effects that are included, the longer the rendering process will take.

12. You will be informed when rendering is complete. The video preview will begin playing.

13. Click on **Finish** again.

14. Don't forget to save your project one last time.

This concludes the Try it exercise for producing video using the Smart Player output options.

Summary

This chapter provided instructions to produce the final output for delivery to consumers using a standard website or video streaming site. You now have a good picture of how learner interactions with your video can be leveraged.

The trend toward visual learning is unmistakable. The interactivity features in e-learning authoring tools have opened new possibilities for teaching how to perform almost any task or subject. Systems to support these rich features are evolving and becoming the norm in the world of e-learning. It will be fascinating to watch as tools, features, and systems evolve in the future to accommodate the transition to more and more visual learning programs.

Of course, video plays a key role in visual learning. If a picture paints a thousand words, a video paints many thousands. Learners are becoming accustomed to learning complex subjects and tasks quickly and openly, sometimes finding good quality video content on the public Internet. This trend encourages educators to pursue the development of video e-learning content.

It has been an interesting and challenging process for me to share with you these visions of video e-learning and the capabilities of Camtasia Studio, stressing the need for excellence and high-media quality, all in support of new trends in education. I am grateful for having the opportunity to become a specialist and being able to share some of these inside tips with you.

Appendix

This Appendix contains descriptions and instructions about the documents and sample project included with your purchase of this book. Also included are references and links to help you as you develop your Camtasia Studio skills.

The Appendix is organized by subject as follows:

- Sample file descriptions
- Sample Camtasia Studio project
    - ° Accessing the sample project
    - ° Instructions to unzip the project
- Samples of design and development documents
- Document templates
- References

Sample file description

The sample files in the following list are included with this book at no additional charge and can be downloaded from either of the following links:

- https://www.packtpub.com/
- https://packtlib.packtpub.com/

If you do not currently have an account, you can create a new free one.

The following table has the description of all of the files included in the downloadable ZIP file.

File	Description
`Sample-Project-Using-CuePrompter.zip`	This is a zipped (compressed) file containing the Camtasia Studio project file and all the assets used in the sample project.
`SAMPLE-Project-Plan-Using-CuePrompter.docx`	This is a sample Word document project plan for the sample project.
`SAMPLE-Script-Using-CuePrompter.docx`	This is a sample Word document audio narration script for the sample project.
`SAMPLE-Shot-List-Using-CuePrompter.docx`	This is a sample Word document shot list (list of clips to be produced). It shows the shots planned for the sample project.
`SAMPLE-Storyboard-Using-CuePrompter.docx`	This is a sample Word document storyboard for the sample project.
`TEMPLATE-Project-Plan.dotx`	This is a project plan Word template that can be used for planning your own e-learning project.
`TEMPLATE-Script.dotx`	This is a script Word template that can be used to create a script for your own e-learning project.
`TEMPLATE-Shot-List.dotx`	This is a shot list Word template that can be used to create a shot list.
`TEMPLATE-Storyboard.dotx`	This is a storyboard Word template that can be used to create a storyboard.

Sample Camtasia Studio project

If you have been following along in the Try it exercises in this book, you would have seen many references to the sample Camtasia Studio e-learning video project featured in the text. Download the zipped project file and refer to it as you move through the book. After the description of accessing and downloading the project file, there are instructions for opening it from within Camtasia Studio.

Accessing and downloading the project files

To access and download the project files, perform the following steps:

1. Log in to your account at `https://www.packtpub.com/` or `https://packtlib.packtpub.com/`. If you do not currently have an account, you can create one.

2. Click on the **SUPPORT** link.

3. Click on **Code Downloads**.

4. Next to the book title, click on the link for **Code Download**.

5. After download, locate the single ZIP file named `Sample-Project-Using-CuePrompter.zip`.

6. Expand the contents using any standard ZIP utility software.

In the expanded folder, you will notice several individual files, including another single ZIP file entitled `Sample-Project-Using-CuePrompter.zip`. This is your compressed project sample file. You can access the files using the instructions provided in the next section.

Unzipping the Sample Camtasia project

Camtasia Studio has a built-in zipping and unzipping utility to be used exclusively with Camtasia Studio projects. This makes it easy to archive, share, and retrieve your projects. Camtasia creates a project file with a `.camproj` filename extension. This single project file contains references and links to other assets used in the project, including audio, videos, and images. Sharing the project file alone, without the linked assets, will produce errors when the `.camproj` file is opened at another location or on a different computer. The error messages will provide a clue to the missing assets by filename and original location, but that won't help you open the project until you obtain access to those additional files.

> The sample project files included with this book were compressed using the Camtasia **Export project as zip...** feature. The best way to access the included project and asset files is to use **Import zipped project...** to open them. The samples were zipped with Camtasia Studio Version 8.4.

The following steps show how to unzip the project files from within Camtasia Studio:

1. Select **Import zipped project...** from the **File** menu:

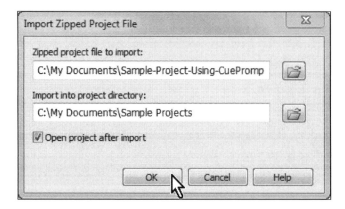

2. For **Zipped project file to import**, browse and select the file you downloaded from the expanded **Code Download** file.

3. For **Import into project directory**, browse and select a location for the sample project files.

4. To open the project, the **Open project after import** box should remain checked.

5. Click on **OK**.

The sample project opens and is ready to use.

Design and development documents

Included with the download are several sample project document files referenced in the chapters of this book. You can use these Word files to create your own project files. Doing so will help you plan and organize your material in ways that will:

*   Make your projects easier to manage
*   Ensure you plan for and get access to the assets you need to complete your project
*   Enable you to enlist SMEs and reviewers to improve the accuracy of your content
*   Provide the basis for gathering your visual and audible assets for the project

These files are compatible with Microsoft Office 2007, 2010, 2013, and Office 365. The files may also be viewed and saved using Open Office (freeware) and Google Docs.

Google Docs samples

Samples and templates are available in Google Docs format at `http://bit.ly/1lBTjN4`.

Document templates

The Microsoft Word templates for each of the four project documents are included for your use as a starting point in planning and producing e-learning videos. For users of Microsoft Office 2007, 2010, 2013, and Office 365, the following are the instructions to save these files as templates accessible from within Word:

- Store the unzipped Word template files (with a `.dotx` filename extension) in the `Templates` directory of your system.

 To find your templates directory, search for all the files with a `.dotx` filename extension. Note the directory where they are stored and store the downloaded template files in this same directory.

- When creating a new file in Word, select the appropriate template in the **My templates** area.

References

There are plenty of tips and discussions available about using Camtasia Studio. A quick search in your Internet browser will produce hundreds of links.

This section provides a few of the best ones and other links referenced in this book. Refer to the following resources when designing and developing e-learning videos using Camtasia Studio:

Description	Link
Describes how to manage Microsoft Office templates	`http://support.microsoft.com/kb/924460`
Bloom's Taxonomy	`http://en.wikipedia.org/wiki/Bloom's_taxonomy`
System requirements for Camtasia Studio	`http://www.techsmith.com/camtasia-system-requirements.html`
Camtasia Studio tutorials for version 8	`http://www.techsmith.com/tutorial-camtasia-8.html`

Description	Link
Instructions and links to install the TechSmith Fuse app on mobile devices	`http://www.techsmith.com/fuse.html`
Download link for free Camtasia Studio library assets	`http://www.techsmith.com/camtasia-library-media.html`
Download link for free Camtasia Studio music tracks	`http://www.techsmith.com/camtasia-library-media-music-tracks.html`
Video streaming and sharing site with limited free storage	`http://www.screencast.com/`
Link to the free CuePrompter script reading application	`http://www.cueprompter.com/`
Link to professional voice-over services	`http://www.voices.com/`
Link to access or sign up for a SCORM Cloud account for testing SCORM packages with limited free storage	`https://cloud.scorm.com/`
Penn State University Learning Design Community Hub	`http://ets.tlt.psu.edu/learningdesign/effective_questions`
Information about the Moodle LMS community	`http://moodle.org/`
Information about Aviation Industry CBT Committee	`http://www.aicc.org/`
Information about the Rustici Software Tin Can API	`http://tincanapi.com/overview/`
Download links for Audacity audio editing freeware	`http://audacity.sourceforge.net/`
View tutorial on creating a branched interactive e-learning video	`http://www.spectorial.com/branching.html`
View tutorial on creating an interactive quiz in Camtasia Studio	`http://www.spectorial.com/quizzing.html`

Description	Link
Example and instructions for embedded video on a web page using an iFrame	`http://www.spectorial.com/trainingsamples.html`
Additional Camtasia Studio e-learning resources	`http://www.spectorial.com/catalog.html`

Index

Series 50
Superimpose 50
Zoom in / Zoom out 50
video teaching 7, 8
video tutorials
URL 61
virtual whiteboard
using 70
visual effects
using 103
Visuals column 50
visuals, laying out
about 87
title, adding 88

W

webcam 58
whiteboard
recording 70, 71

Z

zipped project
importing 78
zoom
applying, to portion of timeline 113
zooming 112
Zoom-n-Pan feature 113
zoom out
applying 115, 116

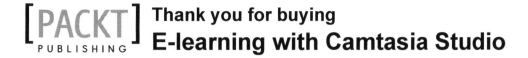
Thank you for buying
E-learning with Camtasia Studio

About Packt Publishing

Packt, pronounced 'packed', published its first book "*Mastering phpMyAdmin for Effective MySQL Management*" in April 2004 and subsequently continued to specialize in publishing highly focused books on specific technologies and solutions.

Our books and publications share the experiences of your fellow IT professionals in adapting and customizing today's systems, applications, and frameworks. Our solution based books give you the knowledge and power to customize the software and technologies you're using to get the job done. Packt books are more specific and less general than the IT books you have seen in the past. Our unique business model allows us to bring you more focused information, giving you more of what you need to know, and less of what you don't.

Packt is a modern, yet unique publishing company, which focuses on producing quality, cutting-edge books for communities of developers, administrators, and newbies alike. For more information, please visit our website: www.packtpub.com.

Writing for Packt

We welcome all inquiries from people who are interested in authoring. Book proposals should be sent to author@packtpub.com. If your book idea is still at an early stage and you would like to discuss it first before writing a formal book proposal, contact us; one of our commissioning editors will get in touch with you.

We're not just looking for published authors; if you have strong technical skills but no writing experience, our experienced editors can help you develop a writing career, or simply get some additional reward for your expertise.

Drupal for Education and E-Learning

Second Edition

ISBN: 978-1-78216-276-6   Paperback: 390 pages

Create web-based, content-rich tools for teaching and learning

1. Create a powerful tool for communication among teachers, students, and the community with minimal programming knowledge.

2. Produce blogs, online discussions, groups, and a media hosting platform using Drupal.

3. Step-by-step instructions in a teacher-friendly approach; creating your classroom website will be an enjoyable task.

Adobe Captivate 7 for Mobile Learning

ISBN: 978-1-84969-955-6   Paperback: 136 pages

Create mobile-friendly and interactive m-learning content with Adobe Captivate 7

1. Explore the various ways to bring your e-learning content to mobile platforms.

2. Create a high definition screencast and upload it on YouTube.

3. Create mobile-friendly and interactive software demonstrations and SCORM-compliant quizzes.

Creating E-Learning Games with Unity

ISBN: 978-1-84969-342-4   Paperback: 246 pages

Develop your own 3D e-learning game using gamification, systems design, and gameplay programming techniques

1. Develop a game framework for a 3D e-learning game.

2. Program dynamic interactive actors and objects to populate your game world.

3. An easy-to-follow guide along with an extensive source code to support and guide readers through the concepts in the book.

Moodle 2.0
E-Learning Course Development

ISBN: 978-1-84951-526-9   Paperback: 344 pages

A complete guide to successful learning using Moodle

1. The new book and e-book edition of the best selling introduction to using Moodle for teaching and e-learning, updated for Moodle 2.0.

2. Straightforward coverage of installing and using the Moodle system, suitable for newcomers as well as existing Moodle users who want to get a few tips.

3. A unique course-based approach focuses your attention on designing well-structured, interactive, and successful courses.

Please check **www.PacktPub.com** for information on our titles

Made in the USA
San Bernardino, CA
07 March 2017